A DISTORTED REVOLUTION

HOW ERIC'S TRIP
CHANGED MUSIC, MONCTON,
AND ME

A DISTORTED REVOLUTION

JASON MURRAY

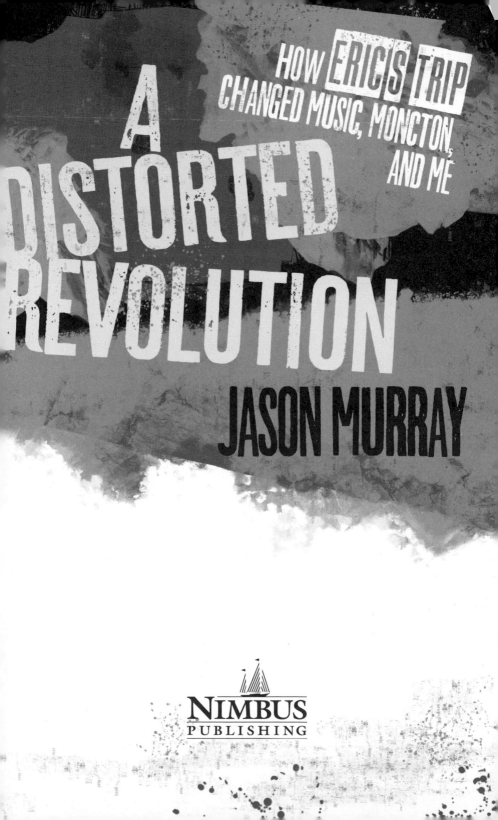

NIMBUS
PUBLISHING

Nimbus Publishing Limited
3731 Mackintosh St, Halifax, NS, B3K 5A5
(902) 455-4286 nimbus.ca

Printed and bound in Canada

NB1242

Cover and insert photos: Ray Auffrey
Cover and interior design: Jenn Embree

Library and Archives Canada Cataloguing in Publication

Murray, Jason, author
A distorted revolution : how Eric's Trip changed music, Moncton, and me / Jason Murray.
Issued in print and electronic formats.
ISBN 978-1-77108-493-2 (softcover).—ISBN 978-1-77108-494-9 (HTML)

1. Eric's Trip (Musical group). 2. Alternative rock musicians—Canada—Biography. I. Title.

ML421.E685M98 2017   782.42166092'2   C2016-908062-5
                                                 C2016-908063-3

Canadä

Nimbus Publishing acknowledges the financial support for its publishing acti-vities from the Government of Canada, the Canada Council for the Arts, and from the Province of Nova Scotia. We are pleased to work in partnership with the Province of Nova Scotia to develop and promote our creative industries for the benefit of all Nova Scotians.

FOR DORIS AND DIANE, WHO TAUGHT ME RESILIENCE.

FOR EACH GENERATION
EVERYTHING COOL BECOMES CLICHÉ

WHAT WE HELD CLOSE
IS OFTEN EXPOSED
AS THE OPPOSITE OF TRUTH

NOT MUCH THESE DAYS
ISN'T FOR SALE
INCLUDING OUR IDEAS
SHAPED BY THE WORLD
TELLING US HOW TO THINK

THERE'S A REASON
WE STILL LOOK TO THE RIGHTEOUS
NO BULLSHIT OR COMPROMISE
WANTING TO BELIEVE TRUE ART STILL EXISTS
AND WE COULD MAKE IT TOO
IF WE WANTED.

CONTENTS

INTRO

Moncton always lacked a real identity. But it had an edge. It was rough and you had to fight to get what you wanted. Nothing came easy for those along the Petitcodiac River. We were born into a long line of people who struggled to survive doing hard labour, in tough industries, during long hard winters. It wasn't uncommon to see packs of men walking out of plants in overalls, lunch cans swinging from their sides, heads and shoulders slouched forward. Those same men would be seen spending their meagre paychecks at the long line of dingy bars along the city's downtown on the weekends. Blue and red flashing lights bouncing off the side of buildings, highlighting the guilt and resentment on their faces as they were put in the back of police cars.

When I grew up, in the 1980s, Moncton was a sea of blue–collar uniformity. Industries came and went, and it took a long time to understand who we truly were as a city. My friends and I got lost in John Hughes movies, wishing we were somewhere else. Moncton had gotten its comeuppance in 1918 when the Canadian National Railway (CNR) set up its Maritime headquarters there. At its peak, over six thousand workers would be employed. Along with the *Eaton's Catalogue* warehouse, a new airport, a meat-packing plant, and a military supply base, Moncton's tide was on the rise for decades. With the construction of the University of Moncton in the early '60s, French and Acadian culture began to flourish and the city developed among the marshlands. But restructuring in the '80s saw layoffs and the closing of major industries. When CNR announced it was shutting down its shops after almost seventy years, Moncton would feel the first of many economic hits. That decade dealt a series of blows. After the military base and warehouses closed, those who stuck around did what they could to raise their families. People soldiered on, heads high, but a grudge developed with time. This chip was passed on to our generation and many of us grew up feeling like the world owed us something.

Everyone was trying to find a place among the growing rich and poor divide. In the '80s they called it the middle class. Nobody was really happy living on the outskirts of the rest of Canada. We lived in the shadow of bigger populations to the east, cities like Halifax, with a port and Navy yards. Then there was the west. Everything followed the Trans-Canada away from the Atlantic: Montreal, Toronto, the Prairies, and beyond. The myth continued to grow about what might be out there. It beckoned every spring and fall.

We were thousands of miles away from the next biggest scene, in Montreal. When you saw or heard about bands doing cross-Canada tours, they always began in Vancouver and ended there. "From coast to coast," they would say. I guess they meant the coast of the St. Lawrence.

We knew how the rest of the country saw us: unemployed fishermen and farmers, rural and backward, trying to make our stamps so we only had to work half the year or seasonally. East of anywhere, people had no idea there were even cities in New Brunswick. They might have heard of Halifax but it was just a barnacle-covered town of oyster eaters and lighthouses. Postcard pictures sold in airports of old-timers in yellow raincoats.

We grew up ashamed of our place. Not only geographically but also our station: lower middle class. A whole generation who grew up in broken homes without direction or guidance. Pissed off, victims of our parents' circumstances. Our city was built on the fuel of that anger. Motivated teenagers trying to prove something to the fathers who weren't around.

By the time I was born, in 1974, kids were sick of these same troubles holding them back. Tired of feeling like the same meat-plant future was in store for them. We all wanted to break free—determined to break out of that mould by somehow embracing what we wanted to move away from. Halifax had a bigger student population that turned over every year, bringing new trends and fashions to the city. It had enough people to attract certain kinds of retailers and shops and keep them there, where most of what Moncton had was the same for generations. New stores tried but people were stuck in the past; they wanted what they knew and had no plans to change or spend more money on something they could get for less at Woolco. Glass windows were covered up and nothing changed in the way people looked or thought for a long time in the streets of the Greater Moncton Area.

The brave few, those with vision far beyond their years, set trends long before anyone was able to see them. Dirty jeans and T-shirts were seen as the uniform of those who did hard labour. My father told me about his grandparents, men and women before them: people who worked with their hands, did physical work, and did not want to get their good clothes dirty at work all day. They wore stuff they weren't worried about ruining, tearing, or getting full of paint or oil. Old work boots, jeans, and black-and-red checkered jackets became our style. Dirtbag chic rose out of not having the money to buy designer and not wanting to anyway. It was an attempt to revolt and find ourselves. Laughed at in the beginning only to be copied the world over.

Moncton had always been a whitewash of grey architecture and weather. Combined with a lack of jobs and prospects, it kept the mood dark and sombre. Some directed their frustrations into art and music. The red-and-black-checkered revolution and working-class sensibility created a do-it-yourself ethos that helped us re-define a community and a generation. Nowhere was this clearer than in our city's music scene. Built on the foundation of punk rock and tearing down the rock star god complex created by the bands of the '70s, the new sound and attitude stripped it all back. From basic jeans, T-shirts, and sneakers to simple guitars and amps, the Moncton scene would help to usher in a genre of music and style that smashed all the pretension from rock and roll. In a time when music took itself way too seriously.

And at the centre of it all a few kids from Moncton, the middle of nowhere. Not unlike kids from anywhere else in the world who feel isolated, bored, and disconnected, trying to find something to believe in. No different from the kids in all the John Hughes movies we watched over and over in basements. These kids decided to pick up a few instruments, write a few songs, and make art for art's sake. In the meantime they gave us all permission to do the same. They brought us all on a six-year journey, a wild ride they called Eric's Trip.

A/

1

SO IT BEGINS

He rolled up in his red VW van, a cooler in the back and a beer between his legs. Shirtless, his muscles were long, hair hanging past his wide shoulders. A sweet, skunky smell made me cough when I stepped inside. The unmade bed in the back was covered with a gold-flecked drum kit.

We took a drive out to the shore, the smell of cigarette smoke and salt water, something I still remember. He talked about music and good bands. He tapped his hands on the steering wheel, using anything to accent sound and rhythm. He turned the radio up and sang at the top of his lungs, hands flailing all over the dash. When people stared he just laughed.

We talked a lot about rock and country, jazz and blues, the difference between musicians and rock stars.

"Like Hendrix, he transcends genres. You can't put him in a box."

"What about Bonham?" I said.

"Same thing, these guys are beyond the labels forced on them by the music industry."

Windows down, my hair whipping against my temples, I just sat back and took it all in.

Often we would stop to visit a wide cast of characters. Longhairs and hippies, chain-smoking castaways living on the outskirts of town. Most sitting around campfires playing music. Strummers and singers, drummers tapping out sounds on the sides of two-fours.

I remember the smell of fresh seafood in the air. Bubbles bursting over a pot with red tentacles spilling out the side. Picnic tables became dinner tables and friends became family, gathering together on warm summer nights. People came from all around with bowls of food. Hugs and kisses from people I'd never met. Homemade dishes, colourful, fresh from gardens, made to be shared while everyone sat close and told stories or leaned in to hear them. I sat watching and listening, enjoying the freedom from school and home life with my grandparents. It was rare to spend time with my dad and rarer still to see him with his friends, so happy.

My parents met young. They tried to make a bad situation work for as long as they could but neither had the skills nor the money to deal with me. The novelty of playing house wore off as their friends were out enjoying teenage life. I became a burden to the world around me and I knew it. The last happy memory I have of the three of us, we were sitting on a couch listening to The Eagles record *Hotel California*.

Before my dad dropped me off at my grandparents', he often gave me what I called a "going away" present. Usually something my mother insisted he buy: sneakers, socks and underwear, a winter coat. On this day he surprised me with something I never expected. He reached in the back and pulled out a big white bag. It was heavy and awkward. He put it on my lap and pulled away the plastic. He never was one for gift-wrapping.

My lower lip began to shake as I saw what others in my grade five class already had. I held it up with both arms extended, mesmerized by the possibilities in its dual tape decks and detachable speakers. I stared at the handle and its options for portability.

"So, do you like it?" he asked. "It's Hitachi, top of the line."

"I love it."

"I also got you some tapes." He handed me another bag but I didn't even open it. I just kept staring at the stereo on the front of the box. "Your mom is going to kill me," he said with a mischievous smile. "She told me to buy you back-to-school clothes."

I got out and walked to the other side of the van, picked up the two bags, and gave my dad a hug. I started walking toward the door on the balls of my feet when I turned and said, "Don't worry, I'll talk to Mom."

The next day at school I had music on the brain. My friends Ian and Ferg told me about new bands and we talked music all day long. I was now plugged into a network of people who traded tapes and recorded them on their dual-cassette stereos. Day after day I made copies of my small library, dubbing and then exchanging my tapes for new masterpieces scribbled with names like Led Zeppelin, Loverboy, AC/DC, and Billy Joel.

I played these recordings over and over on my paper route, getting to know every nuance of the music and lyrics. My collection continued to grow as I took my weekly paper profits and bought more music and blank cassettes at a nearby record store. As my addiction grew, I had to find new ways to feed my habit, so I increased the number of houses on my route. The more subscriptions, the more money. The more money, the more tapes. All my friends were doing it. They were pushing new music on me every day and the peer pressure was costing me a ton.

One morning I was sitting in art class sharpening my pencil crayons when my friend Scott slid a tape across my desk. "Hey Jay, you've got to listen to this," he said. He was wearing a three-quarter-length rock shirt, had blonde streaks in his hair and a way with the ladies. This wasn't the first time he would do this, and I trusted his opinion. "My sister's boyfriend gave it to me, it's awesome."

I thought about his sister for a minute. She was tall with dark hair and very beautiful. She was also in high school. Every time I went to his house she came down to ask how things were at school and tell us how much fun she had in middle school. She also smelt good.

I picked the tape up off the desk. It was bright orange with a black silhouette: U2: *Under a Blood Red Sky*. Great name, great title, and an awesome cover. Sometimes that's all it took. I listened to the tape all night. It was unlike anything I had ever heard. It was live and the singer was full of energy, passion, and pain. I didn't stop listening to it for three days. Walking to school, I got goosebumps from the roaring crowd, the lyrics, and the politics I didn't even understand. I was making an emotional connection, all the way to the bottom of my feet. I felt a surge of energy through my hands and fingers, moving in rhythm to the music. I was also walking quicker, like blood was moving faster through my veins.

Over the next few months my musical interests and knowledge expanded. I discovered all new genres as older brothers and sisters got into the conversation, insisting we listen to their favourite bands and albums: Bowie, The Beatles, Phil Collins, and Prince became new favourites. It felt like my friends and I had just opened a door to a brand new world.

Ian MacDonald was the first person I ever saw in real life with long hair, tight jeans, and sideburns. Six months older than me, he lived five blocks away but it was like he lived in another world. We were both new to middle school but he knew things I was dying to know, mostly about hard rock. His older brothers were all music fans. One loved Rush, the other had tickets to see Led Zeppelin before John Bonham died. They both had huge collections we weren't allowed to touch. But they weren't always home. We would sit and stare at the wall of vinyl and tapes, lined in alphabetical order. Bands we'd heard of but not heard. It was like our own private record store. We used his brothers' music as a jumping-off point, getting to know the music of our past. Rush's first album, Black Sabbath's *Paranoid*, Pink Floyd's *The Dark Side of the Moon*. It was like discovering the cure for cancer in the next bedroom over.

I'd met Ian through Jason Fergusson. He was a fan of all music and friends with everyone. His hair was black and curly, he laughed a lot, and he was always quick with a joke. Neutral when it came to his appearance, he looked like the buddy your mom would love. He was one of my first friends in my grandparents' neighbourhood; I used to see him when I visited my grandparents on the weekends before coming to live with them in elementary school. Ferg, as he became known, was always around. His brother and sister were also big music lovers and encouraged us to listen to everything from James Brown to Devo. We often sat in his basement listening to a stereo he'd won at school. Tape cases scattered, a wide variety of sounds echoing out.

I remember one day we sat at the kitchen table with the portable stereo in the middle. Ferg switched the tape. He pressed play and we began tapping our forks and knives. Ferg's mother turned and looked at us, smiling as we waited for lunch to be ready.

"This is good stuff Ferg. What's it called again?"

"*Exile on Main St.* by The Rolling Stones."

This was one of many tapes Ferg would steal from his brother's collection. We would learn about music from the roots, one cassette at a time.

III

One afternoon, I stayed after school to watch a friend play in a basketball game. As I walked in the front doors, I could hear the squeaking, dribbling, and crowd noise from the gymnasium. Down the stairs, sneakers and school bags littered the floor. I stepped over the mess and then noticed something that looked out of place. Something I hadn't seen before at our school—or anywhere but in books and magazines.

The bright wheels and board graphics called to me. I walked over and saw half a dozen skateboards stacked up together under the trophy case. I picked one up. It was heavier than I expected. The deck was splintered on the sides and at one end. The paint was scratched on the bottom and the grip tape was rough against my fingertips. The wheels rolled fast and I could smell oil in the bearings. I had an old plastic skateboard at home but it was just a toy. I went into the gym determined to find the owners.

I looked around. Classmates and kids from other teams sat on the benches reading and talking. No one looked the way I thought skaters would. I waited around, trying to focus on the game for the sake of my friend who was trying out. I kept my eyes on the door, hoping a group of students would walk out and reveal themselves.

I could feel beads of sweat forming on my forehead. I was uncomfortable in this environment. The whistles, the lights, coaches yelling at kids to do what they're told. I was independent and enjoyed thinking for myself, figuring things out on my own. I also had a bit of a problem with authority. All these students dressed the same, running together in formation, pushing and shoving, trying to beat everyone else.... This wasn't my scene and I was becoming more and more eager to get out of there.

I sat and watched my buddy Phil running back and forth. I never understood the whole idea of shirts and skins. Some kind of adolescent shaming ritual. I made it to the end of the game and watched as everyone shuffled out through the side and back doors. I made my way and waited by the boards. From behind, I could hear a group of voices, deeper and louder than what I was used to. I turned to see a group of boys walking toward where I was standing. I guessed they were in grade eight or nine. They were tall; one had long hair with a plaid shirt tied around his waist, hanging down behind him. His jeans were ripped and it looked like he had drawn on them with a pen or marker. Another had a shaved head and a leather jacket with patches pinned to the front. He wore tight jeans and high-top sneakers. The third guy was wearing army pants and a muscle shirt. It had something written on the front of it: ANARCHY. Must be a band I hadn't heard of. They picked up their boards, threw their bags over their shoulders, and headed out. I stood there watching, mouth open.

That night, I sat listening to music and thinking about the skateboards. Their long, sleek decks and big, colourful wheels offered a freedom I had been yearning for. Having ignored invitations to play team sports and choosing to hang alone or with friends, I saw something very attractive in the act of rolling down the street, self propelled. For the next little while at school, I would watch as these older students, reserved to the other side of the playground, walked by, boards at their side. I had to have one.

III

I spent months trying to find a real skateboard in Moncton. The best thing available in the city was department-store boards, plastic and heavy-wood monstrosities. Ferg found a longboard at Woolco before anyone knew what a longboard was, but I was still on the hunt for what I had seen, the stuff the pros were using.

Friends were going to the States and bringing back skateboard magazines. We had gotten our first taste of *Thrasher* and this opened up a new world to us. Skateboards, music, shoes, style, California: I wanted it all. I had seen boards with names like Santa Cruz, Vision, and Powell Peralta and been everywhere in Moncton looking for them. Nobody had them and nobody knew what they were. I even called a few places in *Thrasher* to see if they'd ship. Most thought New Brunswick was in New Jersey; the rest wouldn't ship to Canada.

I settled for a cheap board from Eaton's. I hated it. Then one day I walked into a local ski shop called Eastern Sports and saw it: the Santa Cruz Slasher. Lucky for me they had layaway. I spent the next paper-route collection weeks gathering my change and putting it in a sandwich bag. I would drop off ten dollars or so every Saturday for months, marking the days on the calendar. In the meantime, I continued listening to and collecting music. I watched the older kids skate in front of the school. Their hair, sneakers, and clothes—even the way they spoke—stood out from everyone else.

The boys and I began taking our cues from them and the musicians we admired. Guys on tape covers with long hair, black T-shirts and jeans; chinos and golf pants—the more patterns the better—shirts with blood and profanity; button-up shirts, blue-collar work wear, corduroy, tight, loose, ripped or not; nothing designer or preppy. Old sports coats with patched elbows acted as winter coats. Fedoras and flat-sitting hats worked, if you could find them. Anything went if it wasn't in style: all second-hand, not in the mall. It was the look everyone else was trying to avoid and we loved it.

Ferg, Ian, and I started searching out thrift stores downtown on the weekends. We found funny T-shirts and plaid button-ups, like we saw old-timers wearing. We liked the kind of attention it brought us. Kids at school thought we were being rebellious. It had become the style to see who could wear the most expensive clothes to school every day; a contest only a few had a chance at winning. We even got made fun of, but we were just trying to do our own thing.

As the reactions continued and people laughed at us for not dressing like them, we got more into it. We looked even harder for offbeat stuff to wear. It was about pushing back against the homogeny in school and it was also about rejecting what we couldn't afford anyway. For my friends and I, there was no appeal to be sitting at a lunch table wearing the same Beaver Canoe sweatshirt as the person next to you.

III

The days moved along and I got closer to my goal of picking up my skateboard. It was a Saturday and I had collected money from my route for the past two days. I took out what I owed and walked downtown to the ski shop. I was listening to The Police, *Synchronicity*, in my Walkman and I could hear my heart beating above the music.

I walked in and noticed they had a few new boards on display: a white one with skulls; a dark blue one with an abstract design.

I told them my name and put my knotted sandwich bag on the counter. The man smiled when he told me my balance was zero and sent one of the others into the back to get my board. It was even more beautiful than I remembered: bright yellow with a cartoon monster carrying a sword. The wheels where big, soft, and green. SANTA CRUZ plastered across the top. It felt like Christmas morning. I took it, said thank you, and walked out the door.

I sat on the bench outside the store and stared at it for a long time. I rolled the wheels and felt the wood under my hand. I could smell the paint, plastic, and urethane. Thoughts ran through my head: friends playing hockey, watching baseball from the bleachers, having no interest in soccer or basketball. I jumped up and began pushing the board down the sidewalk. I felt free. My legs were a little shaky and I used my arms to keep my balance. My left foot forward, I stepped on the tail to try to slow myself down. I was on cloud nine. I couldn't even feel the sidewalk cracks under my feet. Gathering speed, I carved from one side to the other, stopping at a crosswalk. I grabbed the deck and pulled it up to my side.

In the window, I saw my reflection. My clothes, my sneakers, my hat, my board—but there was something missing. I noticed a sign with a white, blue, and red swirl outside a door. I went in and sat down.

"What can I do for you today?" the barber said.

"I want something radical."

III

I ollied a manhole on my street, my book bag lighter than it should have been. I was wearing new Vans just arrived from California. They were not a hit at school with the Benetton crowd. Standing in the schoolyard earlier, a girl I knew had come up and pointed at my shoes, asked me what they were, and told me she didn't like them.

I stood there staring at her. My eyebrows wrinkled.

"They're ugly," she added.

I looked at her ASICS volleyball sneakers. The ones everyone else on the playground was wearing.

"Well, fuck you," I said.

Back on the street I did a few power slides along the road to slow myself down, stopping for a while to skate a curb. I spent some time practicing my moves. I had a fresh new haircut straight from *Thrasher*—one that would probably get me chased downtown on the weekends. It was shaved on both sides and in the back, a wall of hair hanging down in my face. Back and forth trying to learn a few new tricks, I noticed my neighbour hanging out in front of his house putting together a skateboard, his stereo blasting out the window. I walked over to see him.

"Hey Charles, what's happening?"

"Not much, got a new board," he said. "It's a Tony Hawk."

"I see that, pretty sweet."

"Yeah, I like it."

Charles was tall and thin with red hair. He had a paper route too. I admired his home life. His mother was a teacher, his father a doctor. I didn't see his father much. Charles and I hung around after school on our street. On the weekends and at school he spent time with guys his own age. He ordered a lot of stuff from California.

Tools were sprawled across the steps. I pushed some aside and sat on the step next to him, nodding my head to the music.

"What are you listening to?"

"Black Flag. They're from LA."

He was tapping his foot faster and faster. I began to do the same. The songs were loud and fast. I was immediately drawn to the aggression. It was the first time I had ever heard swearing in a song and I laughed at some of the lyrics.

"What kind of music is this?" I said.

"It's punk rock."

Punk Rock. I had heard the name, had seen it in the magazines, and wanted to know more about it. A myth was growing about punk, even bigger than the music itself. I was curious. And now here it was. The music gave me goosebumps. It did something to my brain, made it race, increased my adrenalin and gave me energy. Other music made me tap my fingers and feet or nod my head. Punk rock was instinctive: it hit me in a deep down place. Like the first time I saw a skateboard, I was drawn to it; I knew this was part of who I was.

We skated around Charles's garage for a while. The sun was warm and the streets were quiet. Our boards clacked on the street and the sound of metal grinded against cement. After an hour I grabbed my bag and threw it over my shoulder, making my way toward the end of the driveway.

"Hey Jason, just a sec," he called after me.

He ran inside and came back with a tape. He handed it to me and said I could have it. "This is what all the skateboarders in California are listening to."

I flipped it over. On one side it said BLACK FLAG: THE FIRST FOUR YEARS. On the other in black pen, DEAD KENNEDYS: FRESH FRUIT FOR ROTTING VEGETABLES.

I took my Walkman out of my bag and removed *Led Zeppelin IV*. I put the tape in Black Flag side up. On the upper left hand corner were strange markings I recognized from skateboard magazines. Four black uneven bars. I wasn't sure what they meant but shut the top and pressed play.

The song began with fast, distorted guitar, even faster drums, and then a bass that jumped in like a junkyard dog ready for a fight.

I spent the rest of the night listening to both sides of the tape. The next morning I went to school with a new sense of confidence, like I knew something others didn't. My strut and attitude made my friends suspicious.

"What's up with you?" they said.

"Boys, I have something you need to hear."

"What, did you finally buy *Like a Virgin*?"

We stood passing the Walkman between the three of us, everyone nodding and laughing quietly as if it were some cultural taboo.

After school we made copies and listened to it over and over. The next day, we walked the halls with a new determination and outlook. The sights were the same but the soundtrack had changed dramatically. Those laughing or calling us names were now drowned out in the sounds of anarchy battling it out between the arms of our headphones.

2

IT ALL STARTED WITH SKATEBOARDING

Downtown Moncton was the meeting place for the city's twenty or so skateboarders in the mid-'80s. Everyone gathered at the same spots: Assumption Place, the Edit bank off Vaughan Harvey Boulevard, Highfield Square behind the Sobeys. Kids of all ages, watching and learning from each other. They were from a mix of neighbourhoods and families. Some wore store-bought skate shirts, others made their own. We looked like a band of gypsies, some with long hair and most with ragged clothes, our shirts displaying political and social values:

SKATEBOARDING IS NOT A CRIME, I SHOT REAGAN, and MY RULES with a raised middle finger. Hitting all the spots, being chased by older headbangers and security guards, we'd meet somewhere neutral to talk about new bands and *Thrasher*.

This is where Ferg, Ian, and I found out about a mini-ramp in a guy named Rick White's backyard on the other side of town. We were invited to skate it, so even though we were nervous about going into the neighbourhood we couldn't pass up the opportunity. We'd seen Rick and his friends before and knew who they were, so we decided to skate the long trek to Lewisville in the east end of the city.

Rick White grew up in Lewisville, a neighbourhood near Champlain Place. Though a family neighbourhood, it's a bit tough, with a reputation for not taking crap from anyone. It borders the French Acadian community of Dieppe and the Université de Moncton and has its own rules to follow—especially if you're not from the area. Settled in 1866, Lewisville was mostly known for farming and shipbuilding, with a woodworking factory keeping its small population busy until it incorporated as a village in 1960. The growth of the city and its natural sprawl eventually forced it to amalgamate with the City of Moncton in 1973.

Rick's parents led a quiet life in a small suburban bungalow, just a few minutes from Moncton's downtown. Rick used to put on skateboard contests at the middle school just down the road for the growing number of neon shirt–wearing skaters in the city. Crowds of kids, young and old, would gather to watch Rick and his friends, pre-music, creating art with their feet, hands, and boards. Long before anyone understood tribe culture, we huddled together on the broken pavement of underfunded public schools with ramps we made ourselves, with no athletic training, looking strange, talking weird, and acting out. We were attracted to the loud noise, whether it was the music or the sound of our own voices.

Rick was always a leader in one way or the other. He used to organize the contests, gather everyone together, and was one of the best skateboarders around. He also stood out because he was tall and thin, with long hair and a unique fashion sense. You couldn't walk or skate by him without noticing the art on his T-shirts, sneakers, or grip tape. Even in junior high, you could tell he had talent way beyond his early-teen life experience.

My friends and I were always attracted to creativity. And the first time we ever really witnessed it was in Rick White. While most of the kids at our school were buying forty-dollar designer shirts at the mall, Rick and his friends went to Woolco or The Met and bought two-dollar white shirts and drew their own designs on them. We were blown away—not only by the idea of creating their own style, but by their complete disregard for all trends. It was a very brave thing to do in junior high and we loved it.

My friends and I began doing the same thing. We bought markers and cheap Fruit of the Loom T-shirts and copied the album covers of our favourite bands, taking pride in the fact we created this art ourselves. We also started keeping notebooks full of designs, drawing on our grip tape, and making stickers. Whatever we saw Rick and his friends doing when we had the chance to skate with them on the weekends.

When we got to Rick's ramp that first time, we felt like a gang on someone else's turf. We sat and watched, clapped and cheered. Music blasted from a stereo plugged in with a long orange extension cord running across the lawn to the house.

Wheels rolling along the plywood, trucks grinding coping, teenagers hollering: it was the only place in the world I wanted to be. I thought of my buddy Phil doing drills in the sweaty school gym and was so glad to be here with people who talked like I did.

"Hey guys, do you want to skate?" someone said.

My buddies and I stood, nervous and proud at the same time. We ran up the side of the ramp and waited on the deck. Others dropped in and had their time. I didn't have much to offer but I put my board on the coping. I stepped down and rose to the other side in a 50-50 stance. I rolled back and forth, slashing and grinding, mostly just hanging on for dear life.

I stepped out of the way as one of the older guys moved forward to drop in. He put his board next to the coping and bent slightly at the waist. He watched the skater on the ramp then turned and smiled at us.

"You guys are from the west end? I'm Rick."

We nodded and watched him drop in.

He was tall, thin, and fast on his board. His moves were deliberate. His long hair bounced around like it was defying gravity.

I stood on the side of the ramp, my rite of passage now complete. Ferg and Ian both dropped in and impressed the talented crowd. They were smiling and sweaty, tapping their feet to the music. Everyone was laughing and sharing stories, hands waving, using skateboards as props like we were playing a game of teenage Pictionary.

We spent the rest of the day skating and hearing about other ramps and spots we hadn't known existed. Before we left, Rick told us about his band. He said it was hardcore punk and we might be into it. We told him we liked Black Flag and The Dead Kennedys.

"Then you'll really like this," he said.

"What's the name?"

"The Underdogs."

III

We rolled along, our suburban gang carving and cutting across both lanes of traffic. Cars honked, our fingers raised: skateboarders taking back the streets of our neighbourhoods. Up and down curbs and stairs, we used the landscape like a playground, making enemies of everyone who didn't understand the way we saw the world.

The grip tape on our boards was a mosaic of the teenage boy brain: girls, music, friends, art completely overlooked by those eating out of lunch cans. We were tight-jean-wearing longhairs looking to mouth off, intimidate, and provoke. Since we didn't use deodorant, I'm sure our presence alone kept most people at arm's length.

On a street near our school, we'd discovered a small white jump ramp. We skated by often to see who it belonged to. One day, the sound of skateboarders: a full-on session. They were from the high school, older cats from across town. Music played from their little portable stereo. It was fast, loud, and aggressive. The all-male cast was kicking, spinning, and jumping into the air. Some were even rolling on the ground. My friends and I watched from the curb.

"Hey guys, wanna come skate?" someone yelled.

Two guys named Chris and Ed rolled over and introduced themselves. Chris lived here and owned the ramp. His parents didn't mind the crowd and Ed came over often from Riverview to skate and hang out. They were best friends.

Located right across the causeway connecting Riverview to Moncton's west end, Chris Thompson's house was in a newer suburb, developed in the '70s and '80s around Jones Lake. It was a mix of working-class and professionals, surrounded by army barracks where military families lived, with an English and French school plunked right in the middle.

Newton Heights, as it was once referred to, is now considered Moncton's new west end. Once mostly known for the industrial park and the now defunct CNR Shops, where huge container loads of train traffic passed through the city until the late '80s, it is now known for the city's largest urban park and man-made lake. Until recently it was also home to another large employer, Hub Meat Packers, which closed in 2014. The new west end was also a short skate or bus ride to the downtown. You could often find a crowd of long-haired obnoxious skaters on the number-nine Acadia Park bus heading to the Highfield Square Mall. This stop was a hub for most busses in the city and skaters would gather there and spread out downtown. Highfield Square was known as the "dirt mall"—not as big or well serviced as Champlain Place in Dieppe. It had lesser-known stores with lesser-known brands. Even the food court wasn't brand-name. This attracted a different crowd, alternative types—our kind of folks, no glitz or glamour. It made for lots of fun, especially later at night.

Chris grew up across the street from Bessborough School, one of the first gathering spots for local skateboarders in the area. Like Ed, he met other like-minded music fans at the same skateboard contests in Riverview and at Rick White's events at Lewisville Junior High. He would then hold his own mini skate sessions on the walls, stairs, and jump ramp in the Bessborough School parking lot.

The Thompsons' bungalow, a few streets up from where I lived, would be the same place where Chris, Rick, Ed, and Julie—who we hadn't yet met—would start jamming together and record the first Eric's Trip cassettes. The art of skateboarding and the creativity it inspired transferred itself to music when these guys found and picked up instruments for the first time. None of us were ever going to lean toward organized sports and we all had something to offer the world creatively. It was no coincidence they found each other. None of us liked being told what to do. We were not sheep among the herd in our school packs; we broke out to create our own paths. These paths were starting to intersect all over the city. It would not only redraw the map of Moncton, it would reshape its music in the decades ahead.

Ed Vaughan grew up in Riverview, a tiny bedroom community where families looking for more space and quieter streets with less traffic began to settle. Located across the Petitcodiac River from Moncton and settled by residents of Yorkshire, England, in 1733, Riverview was the result of an amalgamation of the villages of Bridgedale, Gunningsville, and Riverview Heights in 1973. The town's slogan is "A Great Place to Grow," but municipality signs would be tampered with over the years, often changed to "A Great Place to Grow Weed." The town worked hard to form strong ties with its neighbours across the river and connect their youth. They held summer events bringing kids together from Moncton, Dieppe, and Riverview and this helped teens get to know each other. It would play an important part in the future of the music scene years later.

Ed Vaughan was part of a group of young skateboarders who emerged when the town got together to build a skateboard park in a local hockey arena in the summer of 1987. A bunch of ramps spread out over the floor, kids cramming in every few nights, sweating in their helmets at the first chance to skate the kinds of ramps they had only seen on videos or in magazines. Ed became a regular at the indoor skateboard park and it was there he eventually met another skateboarder and future musician, Chris Thompson. Rick White also frequented the Riverview skateboard park and a lot of connections and friendships would be made through the rolling sounds of urethane on wood in the non-ventilated air of the Byron Dobson Arena.

Riverview had its own personality and was primarily known for sports kids, especially hockey players. Ed didn't fit in with the rural jocks on the Albert County streets who liked classic southern rock and country. Kids were already wearing Albert County Liquor Pigs T-shirts handed down from their parents, and there was a rumour of a local headbanger who had a crooked ACLP tattoo on his forearm in India ink, done with a pin or maybe a Walkman motor. These things were not uncommon in the area.

The CAN-USA Games was a yearly summer event that brought kids from Brewer, Maine, to Riverview. It was a large mix of organized sports but when the skateboarding rage of the '80s swept through, it became the focal point of everything athletic. The town set up contests at the indoor skateboard park, attracting anyone with a board and wheels, and bringing the players in Moncton's future music scene together under one roof. From all points North, East, West, and South, across the city and from other parts of the province, skateboarders rolled into the Byron Dobson to compete. Ed Vaughan was a strong skater and did well in the city's first contests. It was here people would find out he was a drummer.

The seeds of Moncton's music scene were being planted at these events, while everyone was getting to know each other and what they had in common. Besides skateboarding, there was another passion everybody was dying to talk about. Word was spreading about who had instruments and, better yet, who was able to play them. Ed had caught the bug in Riverview and he would make a lot of friends quickly over a mutual love of hard, fast, angry music.

III

My buddies and I were stoked when we recognized some faces at Chris's ramp session one day.

"There's Rick."

He was wearing a homemade Underdogs T-shirt; at that time, Rick played bass for them. My friends and I bought a copy of the cassette from Le Disque, a local record store. It was everything we wanted from music at the time. Mid-'80s hardcore punk full of adolescent anger. Fronting this testosterone-fuelled attack was Mike Feuerstack. Dan Boudreau was killing the drums with amazing speed and Chris Foran was shredding the guitar. We couldn't believe this music was being made in our city. We knew Mike and Dan from skateboarding; we would see them at Rick's ramp. They would also be at local skate contests and my friends and I listened to their band on our Walkmans. The artfully made sleeve, a sign of what was to come, would be a photo collage or a handmade drawing, usually from looseleaf, resembling a high-school art project. Most were hand assembled and hand numbered and none were identical. The care and time put into the cover was as much a piece of art as the music itself: no mass production, no concern for sales—in fact, quite the opposite. The whole idea was sharing your art with a handful of people. The Underdogs's *Live at Peggy's Cove* cassette with handwritten liner notes was a prized possession.

All one minute and forty seconds of "No Nukes" gave me politics, attitude, and a place to fit outside of the regular cliques at school. It changed the way I saw things and the way I was told to see the world. I had been subversive, independent, and done my own thing up to this point, but it was about to get worse. I was a skateboarder now and I liked punk rock. It was written all over my face that I didn't give a shit. This was a turning point and would have a huge effect on how I would see the world in the future.

The rest of the day was spent laughing and listening to music. We provided comic relief getting used to the new ramp and falling over onto the pavement. Everyone shared what they knew about punk rock and skateboarding, getting an education in all things awesome. The white ramp outside Chris's house became our new obsession. Some days half the city's skateboarders would be in our neighbourhood to skate. Rick White, Mike Pragnell, Patti Moran, Jeff Edwards: these guys were amazing and we would try to skate with them, but would often simply sit and watch in awe. Better than anything was that we got to sit and talk music with these older dudes. They would even give us dubbed copies of tapes. I remember the day I skated home with a tape I got from one of the guys, , Minor Threat *Complete Discography*. I've never seen music the same since.

Ian, Ferg, and I spent most of our days after school practicing on Chris's ramp and trying to get better. These gatherings were territorial and we wanted to represent the neighbourhood. The boys and I knew we had a lot of catching up to do.

3

PUNK ROCK MALLRATS

We all ended up at Champlain Mall on the weekends. At this age, we were fascinated with two things: the beauty of girls under fluorescent lights, and music on cassettes. Hopped up on Orange Julius, we strutted along in our torn jeans and jean jackets, skateboards at our sides. There was one destination we always looked forward to on the long walk from one end of the mall to the other.

The doorway was covered with posters of shows past and present. The lights were dark and album covers decorated the walls. A guy with a beard stood behind the cash bagging tapes. Another guy in a black T-shirt walked the aisles flipping through cassettes, putting them back in order. The energy was amplified by the music playing from overhead speakers, hair bouncing to the tempo of feet tapping; it moved through the room like a current.

Mark Gaudet was in charge of the punk and hardcore section of the store. He was the reason we, and legions of other teenagers, spent our Saturdays huddled around the stereo, listening to what he played and buying what he recommended. He had long roots in Moncton music and knew all sorts of musicians from headbangers to punks. He was loud and brash and scared me a little. His hair was the opposite of whatever was in style: long, with sideburns down past his chin. His fashion choices were not at all influenced by the stores down the hall. I never saw him in anything but band T-shirts, jeans, and sneakers: he looked like the guy your mother always warned you about. He liked the sound of his own voice but had the goods to back it up. Stories and reputation swirled around him like a big heavy coat, yet he bounced around freely, dancing to the beat of his own drum, spreading knowledge to the next generation of kids like it was his duty.

Mark grew up north of Moncton's downtown, close to the two major hospitals. Another densely populated suburban area where lots of families and kids roamed the streets, parks, and green spaces just above Mountain Road; another working-class area known for its diverse mix of people, houses, and salaries. Located on the edge of Parkton Heights, one of the tougher parts of town, it would be a clash of those looking for fun and those looking for trouble.

Mark found music through his father and older brother. Both were musicians and huge music fans. Since as far back as Mark can remember there was music in the house and he remembers jazz being an early influence. In 1974, at age eleven, he started one of the country's first punk rock bands, Purple Knight, with childhood friend Raynald Leger. Taking their love of Deep Purple, an acoustic guitar, and a broken-down drum kit, they started putting on shows in Mark's kitchen, and they have been playing in the city ever since. Today, Purple Knight is Moncton's longest-running punk band. Their do-it-yourself attitude and love of music planted a seed early.

Mark's grandmother shot their first video on 8mm film. It shows Mark in an Adidas T-shirt beating on drums while Raynald strums away on an acoustic guitar. They sing "Purple Ocean of Hate" in high-pitched, whiny voices while the sound of drums and cymbals crashes in the background. It was pure punk magic from the very beginning, and a sign of what was to come. Moncton was to produce a sound not unlike this primitive, from-the-gut music. Not overproduced, not overplayed or over practiced, just natural, stripped down, and straight to the point, no bullshit.

In 1975 Mark read a story in *Circus* magazine about a New York City band called The Ramones. This is where he saw the word "punk" for the first time. He continued reading about the music and the movement. The long hair and leather jackets were appealing. "I saw a television show called *Don Kirshner's Rock Concert* with The Ramones as guests," Mark says in his farmhouse outside of Moncton, his band room filled with posters and pictures from all his bands old and new. "It changed my life forever." The next day at school, he looked for people who might have seen the show, people he could share the experience with and relate to. Most people thought The Ramones were a joke. Then someone told him about a record store on Champlain Street called Sam The Record Man. The minute he walked in, he knew he had found his people.

At a time when James Taylor and Donna Summer were tearing up the radio charts, the crew at Sam's was playing Devo, Blondie, and Elvis Costello. They were already selling punk records, talking good music, going out after work and vilifying cooperate rock. Mark said he liked this crowd right away, especially after he realized they shared his ritual of listening to music and smoking hash. He would also meet a bunch of musicians here, like him, who wanted to experiment and push music in new directions.

Though he never quite left Purple Knight, Mark would move on to other bands in the neighbourhood. The Punks and The Whore Moans would grow from these streets. They had an attitude and style everyone would try to copy, from jean and leather jackets to DIY recording and underground shows taking shape in the '70s in and around the lesser-known parts of the hub city, and this would play a huge role in the aesthetic of the early '90s as well as how many would come to know Mark, and Moncton, in the future.

The Robins would eventually morph out of this area as well. Row houses, student apartments, and faded jean jackets lending to the punk rock mania that made up the early 80s threesome. Mark never felt Moncton had any less to offer than any other city in the country. He knew there was music in its streets and neighbourhoods and he was determined to mine it.

When Mark started working at Sam The Record Man in 1980, he began meeting other musicians and sharing his interest in making music. It was nice to find a spot where people could gather and that people were just as excited as he was to experiment musically. Nobody was interested in following the Top 40 formula of classic or pop rock in their after-work jams and bands. Everybody was trying to push the limits and bring something authentic back to rock and roll. Some might even say revolutionary.

Holding court on Champlain Street, Mark would order, push, and sell new and interesting music to the legions of young and up-and-coming fans who would make a trip to the store every week. Crowding around, they waited to hear what Mark had to say next—his new obsession, favourite band, album, style, or genre. Those in the know, or wanting to know, would scoop up what he assigned like students from a teacher. Those albums and cassettes would circulate through the scene, getting lots of attention from everyone until the next one got his blessing. Always something new and different.

It wasn't until Sam's moved into the mall that Mark Gaudet reached a new level of fame. Mallrats began hanging around, sometimes all day on the weekends. The music store became the place to see and be seen. If there was a place to stand, look cool, and flick your hair back, it may as well be somewhere you could hear Black Sabbath and listen to Mark tell wild stories about the shows he played. There was no better place to learn and no place anyone wanted to be on a

Saturday afternoon in the mid-'80s than Sam's in the mall. Posters hanging, all the coolest musicians, and people popping in and out with Mark Gaudet yelling out across the store at anyone who came in, "Hey Whoremaster, good to see you." It didn't matter if they were children or seniors, politicians or priests.

Mark's spirit and enthusiasm would lay the foundation for bands to come in Moncton. He would pass on this near-obsession with music, especially with punk and hardcore, to guys like Ray Auffrey, known as Ray 13, and a long list of mallrats; guys and gals who would form their own bands and create the next generation of scenesters.

Following the success of Purple Knight, in 1978 Mark started another band, called The Punks, that eventually morphed into The Whore-Moans. Both bands died out quickly and were more about showing off and making noise than playing music. In 1980, the same year Mark began working at Sam The Record Man, The Robins came together.

A natural evolution of Purple Knight, The Robins the were next generation of punk rock. In 1980 they released a self-titled album, playing basement shows for a handful of enthusiastic fans around Moncton. They made two trips to Halifax and made connections with other bands, laying a framework for a future touring circuit. Heavily influenced by British punk at the time, the trio would become influential in its own right. Mark played guitar in this band, experimenting with the sounds of the emerging hardcore bands coming out of the West Coast.

One of the bands Purple Knight and The Robins would help spawn was Bad Luck #13, which evolved out of a group of likeminded people wanting to stir up shit and revolt against the status quo. Finding good bands and new music on the east coast was difficult so, for people like Mark, getting ahold of the coveted *Maximumrocknroll* magazine was important. It provided information on new bands, new sounds, gossip, and, more importantly, addresses of labels in other parts of the world. It made our isolation a little more tolerable. Add to that the rise of college radio, delivering new bands from the US and the West Coast and giving guys like Ray Auffrey and Ed Markee, the band's founders, all the music they could handle. Canadian redneck arena rock just wasn't cutting it anymore for this group of subversive kids who refused to follow their peers. The members of Bad Luck #13 were all frequent visitors to Sam's and knew Mark from as far back as the '70s. From their garages they created music that was almost theatrical in nature. Never a dull moment, band members were known to lie on the stage playing dead, looking for a reaction. "It was part music, part performance," Ray says, looking back. It wasn't uncommon to see the band in drag, encouraging and antagonizing their audiences to play along, argue, and act out. They didn't spend much time worrying about what others thought. They only cared about the music.

Mike Melanson would join Bad Luck in 1987 as vocalist extraordinaire. His punk rock roots and attitude made him a perfect fit. He would become known as The Man of Bat often dressing up as Batman, and attempted to act out superpowers on stage. He was even known to try and fly. Two other Monctonians, Dennis Marquette and Richard Auffrey (no relation to Ray Auffrey), who had developed a subversive attitude toward mainstream music through the growing influences of duelling language cultures, would join the band later. Fully formed, Bad Luck #13 would play and entertain audiences all over the Maritimes with straight ahead punk rock, during a time when music was changing from hardcore to metal.

Ray Auffrey spent a lot of his early high-school years hanging around record stores and would become part of the next generation of clerks to influence kids in the city. Much like Mark Gaudet at Sam's, Ray was a fixture at independent shops like Le Disque, Room 201, and Blast Off Records.

Room 201 was becoming an important record shop and institution, as it was only a few blocks from the city's largest high school, the same school Rick White and Chris Thompson left each lunch hour. Buying records, chatting with Ray, who was the new guru clerk of the downtown scene, they learned about new albums, new bands, and the bigger scene they would eventually become a part of. Room 201 was the place to go to get obscure and import records. The guys who worked there could tell you about albums you didn't even know existed. They were also instrumental in developing your next favourite band: some local, some way underground.

Small labels from small towns would create a network, through shops from all across the country and the US. These bands did not get big press but would be pushed by local shop guys in the know, like Mark and Ray, who loved their stuff and would do special orders. Music you couldn't get anywhere else was key for angst-ridden tee-nagers trying to be different; those looking for something obscure to impress friends with, or musicians looking to find a distinct sound to emulate. "You can't underestimate the importance of local record stores in developing the scene," Ray says. This exchange between shops helped local bands network and get to know each other. They set up shows and people found each other through posters hanging in the windows.

Ray remembers when all of a sudden there were more shows, more kids, and bands with a new, cleaner version of punk. These bands were riding the wave of homemade videos, MTV, and skateboarders roaming the streets with big shorts, long hair, catchy choruses, and faster tempos. I remember that time well. We started seeing homemade T-shirts around the city. This was during a huge wave of California culture hitting our town. Skateboard and music fashion was in more stores than ever and more people were wearing it than necessary. Our culture was still way under the radar but more trendy than my friends and I liked, we started looking for alternatives. Rick White and his friends never followed the trends. They were always two steps ahead of everyone, on everything. When others started wearing mainstream punk shirts, they would draw their own. Usually bands nobody had heard of. I loved this attitude, the originality.

I also followed their cues. Finding lots of new music this way, also going against the grain. White T-shirts were cheap, so were markers. I also loved the challenge of being creative and trying to draw like Rick. His artwork was already distinctive, even in middle school. You could tell he had talent beyond his years and I wanted to find my own. Ferg could draw without much effort and I had a creative bug. One of the shirts I noticed Rick wearing was for his band The Underdogs.

"The Underdogs were a band people were talking about," Ray remembers. "It's when we really got to know Rick White." They played in basements and a few rec centres around the city. It seemed like everything in the world I could ever want. Their few scattered appearances caught the attention of skaters and punk rock enthusiasts. They were kids experimenting with sound, rebelling against the confines of a system they didn't understand or fit into, even at such a young age. It was reflected in their look, their sound, and their attitude, even if they didn't know it yet. My friends and I understood it, plugged in to it, and became a part of the revolution the first time we heard them: loud, fast, angry, and obnoxious with a pretty decent skill level. The singer's voice was high, because he was barely a teenager and he was screaming. Bare chords leading the charge with furious strumming and drumming. They were teenage angst long before that was a thing. Raw energy waiting to explode. The band came together in Dan Boudreau's basement, with Rick White as the driving force behind putting the band together. Rick played bass, Chris Foran played guitar, and Mike Feuerstack (later a member of Wooden Stars and Snailhouse) sang. The band was known to play parties and skate jams. They were a fast, hardcore punk sound, born out of the skateboard movement sweeping the city in 1987. Their *Live at Peggy's Cove* cassette, with the handmade sleeve and handwritten name and artwork, would set the mould for future tapes to come.

More demos started to appear and there was an increased acceptance of punk and hardcore music around the city. My friends and I began buying local music alongside other punk bands on bigger labels. This idea that people we knew could put out music just as easily as The Misfits or The Bad Brains broke down the wall between "us" and "them." It made us feel like maybe we weren't in the middle of nowhere—and even if we were, we had something of our own to offer.

There was lots of encouragement from shops during this time and nowhere was that enthusiasm more evident than at Sam The Record Man. Ray spent a lot of time talking with Mark and they began to discuss the importance of the local scene; how what was happening in Moncton was as important as anywhere else and there was a need to keep accurate records. Soon after, the two of them began documenting everything music-related happening in Moncton from the early '80s on. Ray has since emerged as Moncton's music historian, having taken pictures of almost every punk show in the city since, and recording the dates and locations of gigs, large and small.

With continued interest came new bands and more shows. Bars like the Kacho in the basement of the Université de Moncton. Dark, smoky, with dark walls and an alternative crowd. It wasn't your typical university sports bar; it had a gloomy edge. The Shipyard was a great venue for all ages and bar shows; it was the centre of the scene in those times. The tradition continued to the Esquire, where people met every weekend, locals hammering it out to wild crowds welcoming the chaos. It was an old watering hole, where you could find husbands hiding from their wives playing VLTs right next to local punk kids drinking cheap draft. Scratched-up pool tables and old wooden chairs lined the room with the same old signs for Alpine Beer hanging on the wall since police raided the same bar in the '70s, busting underage kids for pot and fake IDs. And Ray was there, either playing or taking pictures. A head taller than everyone, he held his camera high, snapping shots of the scene he had helped to create.

Mark and Ray saw something in the culture long before everyone else. They saw the spirit in the kids, the rebellion, the sound, and the look. In this case, pumped up, faster punk with a bit of melody but, in many ways, no different than what Elvis did in the '50s, The Beatles in the '60s, or Led Zeppelin in the '70s: music that went against the grain, tapping into a subversiveness that lives in most of us. And they saw it in the middle of our working-class town.

III

After The Underdogs, Rick White played in another local band called The Forest, with Chris Thompson on drums and Ken Leblanc, another skateboarder, on bass. Ken was dating a girl named Julie Doiron at the time. She was hanging around a lot, and eventually they asked her to join the band. Their sound was experimental, heavy and distorted and influenced by the first Dinosaur Jr album. They had a following and released a few cassettes in limited quantities, but friendships in the band were strained: Rick had a crush that didn't go away and eventually, he and Julie started dating.

Julie didn't live far from Mark Gaudet, though she was ten or so years younger than him. She also went to the French schools, so she ran with a different crowd and culture. The English and French divide in Moncton is real and still exists. When you're young, most kids start to mix at parties, but within the French schools there was no English allowed, so spending time with the anglos was a bit taboo.

Growing up, Julie spent a lot of time with her grandmother, who would encourage her to sing, and even gave her some of her first music, including Blondie and K-Tel records. She grew up listening to them a portable record player. The first record she ever bought with her own money was the *Crimson and Clover* single by Joan Jett and the Blackhearts.

At ten years old, Julie began taking piano lessons and really enjoyed them. Then she found an old acoustic guitar in her basement with a chord book and taught herself to play. She learned what she could, but with competitive swimming now a big part of her life she had to decide where to focus her energy. "I had to choose," she tells me from her home in Sackville, New Brunswick. The decision was a tough one for Julie. She began swimming five or six days a week and stopped playing piano.

By grade seven, Julie had switched to saxophone in the school band and then trumpet. A couple of years later she returned to the old guitar and began practicing again. "My mom bought me a better guitar [a Yamaha] and got me a few lessons," she says. "There was no pressure to practice, it was just for fun." She was happy her parents didn't push too hard, and she figured it out on her own. Spending time with the big wooden box, strumming and sliding her fingers across the neck, she eventually found the chords and how they related to each other. It was a feel thing, something you had to discover on your own. Not something someone could force you to find. Making progress with her acoustic, she set her sights on buying an electric guitar.

It was around this time that Julie and Ken were dating. The skateboarding and music community was growing but it still wasn't that big, and Julie's friendships were evolving. Ken was the first guy in Moncton I ever saw with a mohawk. Not to be mistaken with this generation's "faux hawk," he had the sides of his head shaved and his hair spiked straight up. In mid-'80s Moncton, this was rebellious. This was long before the X-Games, when parents were dyeing their kids' hair pink. A proper mohawk in the '80s was a huge statement. A stake in the ground saying, I am who I am and if you don't like it, F. U. Ken was a part of the downtown skateboarding scene and had a mini ramp in his backyard. People would gather there on the weekends, talking music, pros, and other skate spots. This is where the first seeds of The Underdogs formed, leading to bands like Clarence and The Forest.

Still thinking of trading up, Julie explored the idea of starting her own band and bought a Stratocaster copy. Then she met Rick. Another skateboarder and musician, he was tall and thin, awkward, and shy. T-shirts hung off him like a drape. His hair was growing out and hung in his face. He wore black Converse Chuck Taylors with white laces and drew on everything he owned. When Julie started singing and playing guitar in The Forest, she and Rick spent more and more time together. Eventually, this led to the band's breakup and the end of Rick and Ken's friendship.

When Julie and Rick began dating, he encouraged her to play and sing more. A future band would be built on their teenage romance and its drama. The duo practiced more and put effort in to writing songs. Soon Julie met Ed Vaughan through Chris Thompson and the four of them, Rick, Julie, Chris, and Ed, all began spending more time in Chris's basement. With a 4-track recorder they borrowed from Rick and Chris's high school, they would experiment: turning knobs, tuning down, strumming loud—whatever it took to get the music to sound different. Growing up in Moncton, everyone was tired of the same old shit, of kids trying to fit in, wanting to feel like they were part of a world that ignored them and never came to visit. The band didn't want to fit in; they not only accepted their place on the outside, they embraced it, turning what most were embarrassed about into a look, a sound, and eventually an aesthetic the world would come to admire.

III

As the summer passed, fewer and fewer people were skating after school and on weekends in front of Chris's parent's house. Groups would come and go, and sometimes my friends and I were the only ones to show up. It was disappointing as we were starting to learn new tricks and meeting skaters from all over the city. But there was music coming from Chris's basement. The thumping of a bass drum, distortion and guitar sounds like we'd never heard coming through the amps, loud and soft tones and two voices, a boy's and a girl's, alternating back and forth on songs, sometimes singing together. We loved hearing the sounds, and were intrigued. This was raw, new. We knew Rick and Chris played in bands like Clarence and The Forest; we'd often sit on the curb and listen to them jam. But this was different.

I knocked on the door one day to ask if anyone wanted to skate. I heard a bass drum and strings sing through an amp. People were talking and sounds were thumping through speakers. A girl's voice came through a microphone and the sound echoed as Chris leaned out and waved to the other guys.

"You skating today?" I asked him.

"No, we're jamming," he said.

"Sounds good. Is Rick here too?"

"Yeah, and Ed…. Hey, did you guys want to buy the ramp?"

"Yeah, sure. You aren't planning to use it?"

"No, we won't have much time."

"How come?"

"We're starting a band."

"Awesome. Did I hear a girl's voice?"

"Yeah, that's our friend Julie."

"What are you guys called?"

"Eric's Trip."

4

STUFF'S A-CHANGIN'

ocal bands were now craving new music and everyone was trying
to find their voice. Musicians were experimenting, trying to distin-
guish themselves. Shows like *The New Music* exposed Moncton to
bands nobody had heard of. Guys like Ray, Rick, and Mark would hear
about bands and albums and search them out. It was a rabbit hole no
one minded jumping into. Another great source was CBC's *Brave New
Waves*. The city's underground punk and alternative heads were huge
fans of the show and would listen religiously for the next big thing.
Based in Montreal—tours often hit there and Toronto first—radio hosts
got the goods on the who's who, playing stuff sometimes months or a
year before those of us on the east coast would even catch wind of it.

Unless you read about them in magazines or underground fanzines, it was hard to know who was doing what during this time, pre-internet.

Built on the sounds of Purple Knight's more melodic grooves, Bad Luck's straight-ahead punk rock, and The Underdogs's hardcore, tear-it-all-down jams, Moncton's new sound was starting to evolve. Long winters with nothing to do kept people in their basements and garages playing music. The sound was aggressive because people were angry; it was dark because people were bored and they longed for something more than what they had; it became melodic and catchy because the new generation grew up on Top 40 music.

Rick and Julie played well off each other, and the confines and safety of the basements made for easy experimentation. Recording everything on the cheap, they had the freedom to decide whether anyone would ever hear their music. And they never really expected anyone to. They could put it together as a cassette, CD, or vinyl, or not. This attitude allowed them to be creative for creation's sake. To simply make art as they saw it. Downstairs in Rick's parents' house—a cluttered '80s bungalow with faux-wood panelling and a drop ceiling, littered with Coca Cola bottles, tapes, and knick knacks—was a sanctuary where he and Julie tried new things sonically. Rick recorded everything on a primitive 4-track cassette recorder. As the band listened back to what they played, there was something real, raw, and true to what they heard, mistakes and all. "We were having fun, experimenting with sounds and playing them back," Julie remembers years later. They continued to play and practice for the next few months in relative isolation.

The band's heavy, distorted sounds and noisy guitars were an interesting contrast to the mellow vocal harmonies of Rick and Julie. The loud and soft mirrored the contrasting aesthetic, manic and mellow, they would later project in photos and on stage; the music manifested the mood of those all around them. Grey would be the feeling of the generation, the feeling so many would relate to at the time and how their peers saw the future. Not a ton of hope.

Being fans of early punk and college radio, Eric's Trip saw the potential in putting together their own material. Influential indie bands like Sonic Youth and Dinosaur Jr., who lived and played on the east coast of the US and recorded their own music on small labels, made the whole process feel accessible. For those of us on Canada's east coast, living in a secluded area of the country and the planet, it sometimes felt like it wasn't possible to do the things the rest of the world were doing. But for the band's followers, Eric's Trip broke down that barrier.

In December 1990, Eric's Trip recorded their self-titled debut cassette and put it out at Room 201. The world was sick of itself at the time and music was overproduced, heavily marketed tranquilizers to appease the masses. Bryan Adams, Paula Abdul, and Mariah Carey trying to soothe the pain of the growing divide between the rich and poor, to keep the middle from revolting. The Eric's Trip sound was real and that first cassette was everywhere among those in the music scene around Moncton and New Brunswick. My friends and I were listening to it, like everyone else, curious what Rick and Chris were up to now. Obsessed with punk and metal at this point, these new alternative sounds helped stretch our musical ears even further at a time when we were getting stuck in our ways.

Fuelled by teenage love, Eric's Trip continued to write songs. One of these ended up on the Moncton compilation *Naked in the Marsh* with five other bands, including Bad Luck #13 and Purple Knight. Rick and Chris had evolved from their punk and hardcore backgrounds and Julie's voice added a texture to the music that was rough, raw but catchy. They had connected with the sensitive but angry X generation.

III

"Do you know PJ Dunphy?" someone asked me one day.

"No, who's he?"

"He's a skater from Riverview and you guys look a lot alike."

Separated by a bridge and causeway, Riverview was a short drive or hour skate to new spots and more terrain. There were also schools so that meant an expanded brotherhood of skateboarders and punks in the suburbs. We lived close and often made our way across, making new friends and a few enemies.

A new sound was emerging from across the river and would help balance out Purple Knight and Bad Luck's straight ahead punk with Eric's Trip's move toward a grungier, distorted wave. In different basements, a few miles away, a couple of young music fans from Riverview, Ken Kelley and Steve Hickox, came together as a hard rock powerhouse, eventually touring one end of the country to the other, bringing classic rock, punk, and alternative to a whole new generation. Influenced by Rick White's earlier punk bands, Mark Gaudet's early legacy, and guys like Ray Auffrey, The Monoxides would come together in the halls of Riverview Junior High in the late '80s.

On a cold winter evening, Ken and Steve were hanging out in Steve's driveway. Ken's parents were warming up the car. Smoke was coming from the exhaust and it looked like a heavy-metal video and the dry-ice effect Ken and Steve wanted for their own shows one day.

"Check it out, Ken," Steve said as he stood playing air guitar, smoke rising all around him.

"Looks pretty cool."

"Yeah, it's pure monoxides."

Ken Kelley began playing music by accident. His parents were fans of '70s rock and roll and friends with another couple down the road. Their son, Steve Hickox, would hit it off right away with Ken, talking music and bands. They began playing and practicing in Ken's room, making up songs in the tradition of their heroes. They even began recording to a cassette player just to hear what it sounded like.

Growing up in the suburbs, they were disconnected from the rest of Moncton's music scene. Sounds emerging only a few kilometres away felt like alien messages from another galaxy. Ken and Steve were just two kids sitting in a bedroom, strumming along to guitars, unaware anyone else was doing the same.

Eventually, they met others who sang and played music. Chris Lewis, a future Moncton legend with bands like Iron Giant and Zaum, and Dana Robertson, who eventually helped build the scene and touring circuit with his punk band Hope, talked about what they wanted to look and sound like, long before they all started practising together. And they all learned about the scene the same way we did, from Mark Gaudet at Sam's.

One day, Ken's sister asked him if he ever thought about playing the drums. She said maybe he and Steve could start a band. He didn't want to copy Steve anymore and nobody else played drums, so he took lessons and practiced in his grandmother's empty house next door. PJ Dunphy lived down the road from Ken and Steve. He grew up skateboarding and was into a huge variety of music. PJ joined the band as singer, and Dana on bass. Derek Robichaud joined when PJ switched schools and bridged the gap between Moncton and Riverview for everyone. Derek brought years of backwoods picking and grinning to the band, along with some heavy tones and musicality. Steve would eventually make his way to the front as singer and PJ took his rightful spot on the four-string.

When they got together, their music influences began to blend like a pot-au-feu. Old, deep traditions in classic rock—bands like Kiss, MC5, Grand Funk and Cheap Trick—mixed with new aggressive '80s punk rock and heavy metal, the likes of Black Flag, Metallica, Minor Threat, and Megadeth. But even their early tunes were steeped in melodic pop-rock songs, even if it was loud and heavy. They may not have had any real professional ambitions starting out but they knew what they didn't want to sound like. There were a few lineup changes and PJ would come and go, but his heart and gut were with the Monoxides. "I always wanted to play music," says PJ, now forty-two, from behind the drum kit in my basement, where he and I jam after late-night skateboard sessions. "From the first time I heard Cheap Trick, I became obsessed with it."

PJ's connections in junior high and skateboarding helped him meet others from across the river. He also knew Mark Gaudet. The Monoxides played their first show in Irishtown with Purple Knight and Bad Luck #13 in March of 1990. A few shows later, they would play with another band making a name for themselves, called Eric's Trip.

III

Ray continued to watch the scene grow and encouraged local bands. He watched in amazement as the Eric's Trip's cassette continued to sell all across the province. The music struck a chord with locals and a growing legion of fans beyond the city. He began hearing a more distinct Moncton sound and seing something he didn't think he'd ever see: punk rock and alternative music becoming accepted by the mainstream. New faces were coming into the store and asking for Black Flag, and Nirvana's *Bleach*. It was the start of a revolution.

"Some days, we couldn't get albums out of boxes before they would sell," Ray says. "Something was definitely happening."

Ray thought it was strange the first time he sat in a bar and heard harder music playing on the stereo. He was used to hearing classic rock and radio-friendly fare. Now he was hearing Social Distortion, Bad Religion, and Sonic Youth. It was good to finally have people recognize what he and his friends had known all along.

But not everybody was as open minded. "New" punk rock and alternative music enthusiasts were taking the aggression and energy a little too far. These were also some of the same people who used to make fun of "us" for listening to these bands just a few years or even months before. People were starting to say punk was the next big thing even though none of us wanted to believe it. It had always been under the radar, mostly ignored by the mainstream, and we liked it that way. Nobody could see the huge wave growing behind bands in the west, with bands like Nirvana, Pearl Jam and Soundgarden, and the impact it would have on the pent-up frustrations of a generation.

I could see a movement happening in the hallways of our high school. Mostly on the front of the T-shirts worn by the cool and not-so-cool alike. Our little culture of punk rock and skateboarding cool had become mainstream and cliché. We didn't want jocks and cheerleaders listening to our music—we listened to it because we didn't want to be jocks and cheerleaders. It became a bit of an identity crisis for some, like my friends and I. Those who wore Ramones and Dead Kennedys shirts started wearing them inside out or simply wore black T-shirts, not wanting to associate themselves with "the trend." We had spent our whole lives trying to find our place, feeling like outcasts, and then suddenly the captain of the football team shows up at a party wearing a Sex Pistols T-shirt, saying he loves punk rock. It wasn't like we were going to run out and buy a Patriots jersey and say, "Hey, we're taking back sports."

Some retreated to harder, more obscure bands. Some got turned off from the sound altogether. In the meantime, Moncton's diverse scene had everything from hardcore to metal to Francophone rock. During this period of change, in fashion and music, Eric's Trip was still doing their own thing, experimenting with more melody, mixing it with heavy distortion and acoustic strumming. Ahead of the curve and in their own little bubble, the band forged ahead. Rick had a vision beyond what was happening around him and the sound was evolving to suit their own ideas, not following any trends locally or beyond.

The band laid low and spent time practicing and writing songs. Music was changing and people weren't sure anymore what the future held or what they wanted from their favourite bands. Driven by a quality barometer that could only be measured against bands of the past, Rick kept writing songs. The connection between Rick and Julie was strong and their songs were about young people in love. Chris Thompson and Ed Vaughan were taking up the rhythm section and creating a tempo that was smooth and hypnotic with just a little bit of noise.

Eric's Trip was becoming an underground sensation with tapes bought and sold, traded and dubbed at our school and others around the city. Both shy and quiet, Rick and Chris would wander through the halls, disappearing at lunch and after school. I'd catch sight of them rolling away on skateboards, Rick's long hair blowing back against his jean jacket.

III

The audience for Eric's Trip's first show on Earth Day 1991 was an odd mix. On stage, Rick, Chris, Julie, and Ed became different people: confident, enthusiastic, engaged, full of energy and life. The sound bounced off the glass and hit the marble flour. Kids filled the lobby and a large crowd spilled out in front of the building. Rick had hurt himself skateboarding and looked feeble and frail, putting his guitar around his shoulder, singing quietly as the crowd stared in wonder. Then the song kicked in and he fell to the floor in an electric flurry of noise and energy, like he was possessed.

Julie had her back to the crowd for a while. She was shy, her head down. The stage was low and people were struggling to see the band over the heads of adults wearing sports coats and ties. The music was loud and fast. "The amps were turned up, full of distortion to hide mistakes," Julie remembers. There were people skateboarding in front of City Hall. It felt like the outcasts had taken over the world. Kids with long hair and shaved heads, jean jackets with patches, and white cotton T-shirts with homemade designs were walking among politicians. As the closest thing we had to a punk rock band was playing to moms and dads, we were doing hand plants on boards with FUCK written on our grip tape. Half way through the show, Chris Thompson started smashing his Rickenbacker bass against the floor. People were in shock. The show ended with Julie's glasses flying off and smashing in a dramatic crash.

Nobody knew what to make of it, but to my friends and I it felt like a turning point. There was a cultural shift happening, an acceptance of the things most people hadn't understood before. Heads had nodded in the crowd, feet had tapped where they otherwise would have told guys like Rick and Chris to turn their music down, that it was noise and too loud. The hard rock '70s and punk rock '80s had prepared people for this. The ties of the world were being loosened and there was no going back. Eric's Trip had made an impression nobody expected and it was just the beginning.

The band played more shows in Moncton the following year and continued to write songs. Their popularity was growing and they had a buzz, attracting all different kinds of people. Being able to blend and mix with those who felt shut out made us all feel great together. These like-minded people made us less judgmental and we felt less judged because we began to realize there were more outcasts than not. Hundreds of us would sit and talk about our experiences and how much we related with the music. Bands formed, everyone got behind them, and the spinoff went from the basements to the world. It was exciting to finally have a local band to latch onto to. We felt like Moncton was finding its voice.

I enjoyed these gigs on the weekends. Baggage was not welcome in such an honest space. Julie's voice melted away any stress. It was soft and warm against the heavy distortion of guitars. The light and dark, harsh and mellow, balanced out the rest of the band and created just the right blend. Skateboarders, punk rock fans, music nerds: at the concerts everyone felt relaxed and comfortable in their own skin, nobody feeling like they had to be anything they were not.

My T-shirt collection was becoming a diverse mix of colours, art, and musical interests: a white one with four black bars, the iconic symbol of the times, summing up everything about simplicity in music and in life; a grey one with Mr. Cash, a young country legend playing guitar and giving the middle-finger salute. But a limited run, silk-screened drawing of Rick White's early interpretation of Eric's Trip was the one I was most proud of. It reminded me of the grip-tape art Rick used to draw on his skateboards. Long, thin, dark figures, sometimes with no eyes, sometimes with large ones, long hair, standing among trees or with a swirl for a background. I wore my shirt like a badge, like something I earned growing up skateboarding in the rough Moncton neighbourhoods. It was a mild fuck you to those who stood in line, maintained the status quo, and hoped to achieve by following the rules set out before them. It was a symbol of our thing, and we wouldn't let it go without a fight.

5

"TWO LIGHT BULBS AND A BUNCH OF HAIR"

M y friends and I were stoked that the soundtrack of our lives was
being played by those we knew. Our Walkmans shook with dubbed tapes with hand-drawn pictures of bands promoting their
own music. Bands from Halifax (Sloan), Montreal (Voivod), and even
California (Dead Kennedys). All the punk tapes we listened to were
pieced together, never packaged right, sometimes hand-numbered with
notes or stickers inside. Early punk labels still relied on networks of
people to get their cassettes out there. So we thought words scratched

out from the film of newly processed pictures, and local addresses written on the back and folded around the inside of a cassette sleeve— the tabs on top of each tape broken so as not to erase or dub over them—was normal. We understood this DIY attitude and aesthetic. It was the same reason our friends made music, to connect on a personal level with their fans. These demos and albums were also very cheap. Nobody had invested any real money in creating them, and so they sold them for $5. A price everyone could afford.

But things were changing fast, and we weren't sure what to think of it. Our place on the fringe was now becoming cool. With the interest in punk and indie music, the hierarchy of high school was flipping. The cool kids were becoming the outcasts and the outcasts were becoming the cool kids. It was completely unwanted and unexpected; those on the outside were there for a reason: they didn't want the attention.

In April of 1991, ahead of their first show at Moncton's City Hall, Eric's Trip had released their second cassette, *Catapillars*. Recorded live in Chris Thompson's basement, this aggressive-sounding seven-song art project is mellowed by Rick White's honest lyrics and near-whisper tones. This is a band in search of something greater. Acoustic drumming, screams, and tambourines were brave for this time and you could hear the beginnings of a sound that fans near and far would eventually relate to.

Unfortunately, not everyone was happy with drummer Ed Vaughan. His focus had shifted to other things and the band was no longer his number-one priority. While the other members were putting all their energy into Eric's Trip, he was missing practices and spending more time with his girlfriend. Before a show in Fredericton in September of 1991, the band asked Ed to leave. They played the show with Chris on drums and Julie on bass. It was time to look for a new drummer.

A few months later, they released their third, eight-song cassette, *Drowning*, their last with Ed Vaughan on drums. Again, the music was recorded live in Chris Thompson's basement and the sound, although experimental, was more focused. Julie can be heard doing more backup, coming out of her shell as a singer and guitar player. The sound is still heavily distorted, the seeds of full-on psychedelic rock.

Around this time, Rick began to talk to Mark Gaudet about joining the band. They were feeling each other out. They knew one another from bands, the music scene, and Sam The Record Man. Mark liked Rick's other bands but wasn't sure about the direction of this new sound; Rick knew Mark was a killer drummer. Neither was sure if it was a perfect fit. Mark had jammed with Eric's Trip one time, in September of 1990: two songs in Chris Thompson's parent's basement in the city's west end. The band started with a sped-up version of Neil Young's "Keep on Rocking in the Free World," and followed with a song Rick had written. Mark listened for a minute, heard the general idea, and then added his flare. "It was set in sixteenth-note beats," Mark says almost thirty years later. "It couldn't have been more perfect for me."

But time had passed and the band continued with Ed, while Mark played in his own bands and tried to figure out the sound Eric's Trip was going for. He wasn't always sure about new bands and liked to think long and hard before trying something new. At the end of September 1991, Mark was talking with Rick after a gig. He told Rick he now "got" the band and was a fan. A month later, Mark joined Eric's Trip. With all his background, history, and knowledge, Mark brought more than just steady rhythm to the music. He gave Eric's Trip credibility and muscle. They were now a solid foursome.

Mark was glad to be in an ensemble where he was not the only one responsible for looking after the day-to-day affairs. He was happy to sit back and play drums and contribute when asked. The four members were now taking things a bit more seriously, working on T-shirts, artwork, album covers, and more songs. The vibe between them was strong and they were all finding multiple ways to express themselves, whether it was taking pictures, making music, painting, or drawing. They even started looking for a manager and talking about next steps for the band.

In December of that same year, they recorded their first cassette with Mark on drums. The ten-song *Warm Girl* project would produce future songs for Sub Pop, an independent record label based in Seattle who would later approach them. The music was tighter, on-point, and the rhythm section provided a steady heartbeat for Rick's continued experimentation. They even covered Madonna's "Open Your Heart" in a punk rock tribute to making good songs great. *Warm Girl* began to convince others, and the band itself, of Eric's Trip's talent and potential. A month after recording, they played their first show with Mark, at the Kacho.

The band soon heard about a guy named Peter Rowan who was managing Sloan, a Halifax rock/power-pop quartet and the first band of our generation to be signed by a major record label, spreading their alternative sound across the country. After seeing Rowan on *City Limits* talking about his record label, DTK, Eric's Trip sent him a cassette in an envelope with Rick's signature art. Peter remembers getting it and seeing the artwork. "The envelope stood out," he says. "Then I pulled out the cassette, *Warm Girl* I think." Halifax's sound at the time was more poppy. Moncton was known to be heavier. "My first thought," Peter remembers, "was 'holy shit.'"

There was a lot of excitement around Halifax at this time. The term "Seattle of the North" was being thrown around with the rise of local Sloan. The music scene was hot and bands were getting noticed. Sloan's *Peppermint* was attracting a lot of label attention from some of the music business's biggest names. Peter Rowan organized a show in February and invited Eric's Trip to come to Halifax. Meanwhile, Chris Murphy of Sloan was dubbing and passing the *Warm Girl* cassette around to everyone he knew.

The show was booked at Gottingen Street's Club Flamingo in Halifax's North End. An all-ages venue, it was another dark, dingy spot, and served the punk, metal, and alternative bands of the time perfectly. That night, it filled with the who's who of the Halifax scene— and they made a racket. "It was two light bulbs and a bunch of hair," Peter says. The band played hard, thrashing around on stage. Well into the show, Chris Thompson turned and snapped the neck of his bass. He looked shocked and annoyed. Somewhere between adrenaline and anger, he decided to smash the rest of the guitar against the stage, ending the show and stunning the crowd. People left with their mouths open, intrigued and completely amazed.

After the performance, Peter decided to start working with Eric's Trip and offered to manage them. In late March of 1992, the band headed to Halifax again to record with Terry Pulliam, who recorded Sloan's *Peppermint* EP and had seen Eric's Trip's Flamingo show. They recorded a few songs to be released by a small Moncton label called N.I.M. The *Belong* 7" would only include four songs on the original. Rick would record a couple more at home and make it into a five-song album, limitations the original pressing didn't allow for.

Peter and his business partner, Chip Sutherland, told the band they wanted to release an Eric's Trip album under Sloan's label, Murderecords. They would record the *Peter* EP on cassette and CD with Murder, but not before touring around the Maritimes that summer, opening for Change of Heart, an alternative-sounding band from Toronto, who were loved by the college radio circuit and Sloan. Soon after Rowan's offer, he received a call from Joyce Linehan, a Boston-based east coast rep for Sub Pop. She had heard a cut from Sloan's EP and was interested in seeing them play. She made a plan to visit but had to postpone. When she called back, around August, Rowan told her Sloan had already signed, with DGC (a Geffen company that features well known artists like Nirvana, Sonic Youth, Beck and Hole). Planning to come to Nova Scotia anyway to see relatives, Linehan asked if there was any other talent to see.

Rowan set up a showcase at The Double Deuce, which had just opened that year on Hollis Street, for Eric's Trip and the pre-Jale band Tag. Known for low door prices, a mixed bag of college students, lowbrow patrons, and loud raunchy guitars, the Double Deuce was certainly instrumental in moving the scene forward. The show went well and Linehan was impressed. She sent Eric's Trip's music to Sub Pop founders Jonathan Poneman and Bruce Pavitt. The duo wasted no time in offering the band a contract, a slot at the Vermonstrous Music Festival, and an opening gig for their long-time heroes: Sonic Youth.

For Eric's Trip, the deal felt overwhelming. They worried about not having creative control. They were used to recording their own music, doing what they wanted and presenting themselves on their terms.

"It wasn't about money," Julie explains. "We just wanted say." The
Peter EP was in the works to be released on Murderecords and the band
liked the idea of working with a Canadian label. They also didn't want
the pressure of having to produce for a company with high expectations. They didn't accept the offer.

Eric's Trip played the Vermonstrous show in October of 1992—by
far the band's biggest—with Sloan, who were riding the wave of their
hit "Underwhelmed" after signing with Geffen Records. Afterwards,
Poneman and Pavitt of Sub Pop offered Eric's Trip a new deal. It gave
them more creative control, allowing them to record everything themselves, the way they had always done it. There were no huge expectations to tour, record, or do press; they could keep things simple, with
the emphasis on the music. They accepted, becoming the first Canadian
band to sign with the American indie label.

III

Formed in New York City in the early 1980s, Sonic Youth would help
produce some of the east coast's early punk and alternative rock. They
have been credited with creating the east coast sound in many ways.
This new music had drifted up the airwaves along the Atlantic seaboard
to cities like Montreal and Halifax, where it eventually got played on
influential college radio and had a profound effect on bands like Eric's
Trip. And now Eric's Trip was opening for them in Toronto.

Worried about their new exposure and the upcoming show, Rick
decided he should change the band's name, which had been taken
from a song off Sonic Youth's inspirational 1988 double-LP *Daydream
Nation*. Rick was convinced the band would not allow them to use
the name "Eric's Trip" now that they were signed to a major label.
They also didn't want to be associated with another recording act. But
after meeting and playing with Sonic Youth in Toronto, they decided
to keep it.

Sonic Youth co-founder Lee Ranaldo remembers hearing about Eric's Trip in the early '90s, when people started telling him about a band named after one of their songs. Then, they got a chance to hear them. "They had a very authentic sound," Ranaldo says, "with grungy guitars." He remembers playing with them in Toronto and Mark Gaudet asking about the name. Sonic Youth were flattered and had no problem with it at all. Ranaldo recalls Eric's Trip had a very unique Canadian sound—"a cool pop-song feeling"—and a unique spirit and energy on stage; he felt they were tapping into the movement of the day.

Peter Rowan, too, remembers the night in Toronto very well. Eric's Trip played a quick, short set and everybody was nervous. The place was packed and the crowd was super excited. Nobody knew who the opening band was, but people were into it. "Then I saw Thurston Moore at the side of the stage, watching," Peter says. "It was pretty exciting."

It was an interesting time for four friends from Moncton: opening for a band they looked up to, had named themselves after, and whose sludgy, lo-fi, experimental sound had a huge influence on their own. Like Rick and Julie, Thurston Moore and Kim Gordon were also a guitar/bass-player couple in a band, using their young love/life experiences as muse to fuel their punk rock drive. Gordon also led the Riot grrrl movement in the early '90s: a new generation of feminism and girl power led by strong women who took charge of their image and used it against the stereotypes holding them back.

But adolescent love proves hard and Rick and Julie had some tough times during the fall and early winter of '92. There was a sense right away that Rick did not like the attention Eric's Trip was getting. The rest of the band enjoyed the recognition, the momentum, and benefits of working hard, but Rick was beginning to resent it already. This made for interesting creative times. Rick went deeper into his own thoughts, moving further away from the mainstream, and Julie did her own soul searching. Out of frustration with Rick, during a short-lived breakup, she produced her first solo project, *Broken Girl*. "I had some songs I wanted to do on my own," Julie tells me during a phone interview. "Stuff I wanted to try."

There was an air of rebellion floating around that year. People were trying to hang on to strong ideals. "Selling out" was the catch phrase of the moment and some wondered if going to a big label was the right choice for Eric's Trip. This came from kids who had only talked about doing something great and interesting but had never actually gone for it. It was a long-standing struggle in the punk rock/indie world: modesty versus having your music heard. Eric's Trip wanted to get their work out there but on their own terms. Authenticity was key. They were looking for the magic that happens when four people step up on stage and all those other things are stripped away. The moment when everything works and you connect as musicians with a crowd. It's not something you can practice or need thousand-dollar instruments or huge record labels to achieve. This was what Eric's Trip was trying to capture in their recordings: the power of the live show. The thing people connect to and want to share with others. The reason fans all over the world go to shows every night, in every city, in dingy bars, huge fields, and stinky hockey arenas.

III

Eric's Trip was starting to play more shows around the city and the Maritimes, and my friends and I went to see them whenever we could. These shows were still small, intimate, and important. They were our thing, an extension of the lives we had created when we chose skateboarding over organized sports. With the rise of Nirvana's *Nevermind* and the explosion and acceptance of alternative music, we felt like we still had these shows, these bands, and these likeminded people. Most of us were trying to figure out our lives and how we planned to fit into them, what side of the line we were going stand on. This meant something to us then. Still does.

The weekend often started right after the bell rang on Friday afternoon. Everyone had a mission between the time school ended and when the party began. Some went home to clean themselves up; others gathered their best gear so they could last outside in the elements as long as necessary. It was a given we would be in the woods somewhere. House parties were on the decline and with the amount of people who liked to gather together, especially before or after a live music show, the woods, away from everyone else, was the best place to go.

You could often smell the smoke before seeing the fire as you walked down the trails leading into "the fort," a clearing in the woods where everyone gathered to drink and smoke pot. Surrounded by trees, secluded in the middle of the neighbourhood we grew up in, it became a place where all the problems of high school didn't exist. Jock, jerk, nerd, nut, cool, kook—it didn't matter on Friday and Saturday nights. The common thread of music brought everyone together.

Stereos arrived fuelled by batteries stolen from other appliances in the houses of those desperate to share their soundtracks. Even the quiet ones sang at the top of their lungs, high on beer and homegrown, arm in arm with those they hadn't met ten minutes before. Tom Petty to Coltrane, Bad Religion to The Doors, we never knew what we were going to get. We were open to anything and everything; it was all education to those of us with an open mind. We loved music and music lovers, and welcomed friends with mohawks and mullets.

Trains of people came and went up the paths, people shouting and throwing beer cans at each other. Trees swayed back and forth, dividing the moon into thin little pieces. A chorus echoed from those sober enough to keep singing. A dog barked in a backyard just beyond the treeline, the only other sound the buzz of the streetlights. The road looked grey from all the artificial light reflecting off the asphalt.

The windows were covered, nothing visible through the windshield. The last time I checked there were only a few cars in the parking lot, but time was lost in the bubble of the smoke-filled haze inside my buddy's two-door Honda. Music was playing low, but I couldn't make it out. My lips burned, then my throat, as I drank from a heavy jug of rum being passed around. Somebody held out their hand and I took two purple pills that looked like pencil-crayon leads and put them on my tongue.

I turned up the stereo. It felt like the music was coming right out of me. The beats, the bass, the strings vibrating off the guitar. Somebody laughed. Between puffs off a joint I tried to keep it together but the more I tried not to laugh, the more my eyes watered. Then the guitar grabbed my attention and brought me back to reality. We sat, intensely, listening to the *Warm Girl* cassette. We were transfixed as the last of the joint went out the window.

I opened the door and the parking lot was full. People were standing outside the front doors and a line was forming. We cleaned ourselves up and began the long journey from car to show. My head full of chemicals, body full of rum, eyes barely open from the weed, I felt my jean pockets for the essentials. Bottle. Money. Joint.

"Yeaaaaaah!" someone yelled as we walked in the door.

I raised my arm in a fist. The only thing I could do in my wasted state. I heard the rumblings of music and thought this might be the greatest night of my life. Long-haired, sneaker-wearing denim demons were everywhere. Air guitar abounded with some fingering at their jackets, keeping time to the music. Others stood bowlegged, one arm in the air, digging at the imaginary pickups, trying to get every sound to resonate out of the wannabe wood grain they were convinced was in their hands. I loved it all. I was fascinated by the back patches, the people, the commitment.

My body was tingling. Lights were bouncing off everything around me and my mouth was hanging open as I rubbed my hand against my skin. People were yelling and singing and jumping up and down.

When Eric's Trip came out, my brain turned to slow motion. I watched and heard every note I'd studied in my headphones. Heads were swaying, people happier than I'd ever seen them. You could smell the sweat. There was a community and enthusiasm, something they could never create in school. Four people on stage and a sea of people singing along like nobody was watching.

B/

6

LOVE TARA

School is becoming a real chore. The only thing keeping me going at this point is beer, girls, and music. I've quit and been kicked out a half dozen times since middle school and I'm struggling to keep it together. After continued problems, missed days, and issues with my attitude, someone makes me an appointment to speak with a guidance councillor.

I walk into the office, take a deep breath, and stare at the bookshelves. The rows of university pamphlets and course books make me regret walking through the door.

"Mr. Murray, how are you?" A tall man in a dark suit holds out his hand and shakes mine. "Come in and have a seat."

"Thanks."

"You haven't been here in a while I see, not since you arrived here in grade ten."

"Sounds right."

"So, how are things going?"

"Not bad. Things will be much better in June."

"Why's that?"

"School will be over...."

He laughs as he flips through my chart, going back and forth from page to page.

"You've got some good grades here. Did you apply to any universities?

"Just one."

"Why just one."

"I don't know."

"What if you don't get in?"

"Then I guess I'm up the crick."

He wrote a few things down in his notes. I was starting to lose patience with this father-and-son talk. I was leaning my head back now hoping this would come to an end.

"So what do you think you want to do?"

"Don't know."

"What are you interested in."

I took another deep breath. I looked at the posters on the wall. Army recruitment, Government of Canada, Bank of whatever.

"Nothing that I can see."

"How do you want to spend your life?"

"I'm not sure."

"Why don't we do this. Could you write down, in detail, something you don't want to do?"

"I'm sure I could fill a book with the things I don't want to do."

"Good, from there we'll try to figure out which direction we should go."

"10-4."

I spend the next class pretending to be working on modern history but I'm writing the thing I fear the most.

A windowless office, covered in fake-wood wallpaper. A corporate calendar with pictures of local outdoor photos hangs on the wall: old barns, ducks in a pond, tractors with big tires driving down old country roads. Shag carpet underfoot, the most heavily used areas a little shorter and lighter from years of going to and from the photocopier.

A SALESMAN OF THE YEAR 1998 plaque hangs beside my high-school diploma. Both are dwarfed by my OFFICIALLY LICENSED TO SELL INSURANCE IN THE PROVINCE OF NEW BRUNSWICK certificate. A well-used coffee maker sits on an end table.

My pine, pressed-wood desk is beginning to tilt to the side from the weight on top of it. I have a multi-line phone, a stacked set of baskets for in- and outgoing files, and a bowl of hard candy for clients. Business cards sit in a neat row in their holder, next to my Rolodex, and when I catch a glimpse of myself in the mirror, I see a dark, rust-coloured suit with a blue tie and black faux-leather shoes cracking along the seams. Walking over to the water cooler to fill my SUCCESS coffee mug, I take a hat hanging off the five-point-buck bust, left behind from the previous tenant in my rented mini-mall office, and cover my balding head before kissing my hand and touching the crucifix over the door.

"Heading to Arby's," I say to my administrative assistant, who's just my mother. "I'll be back at 1."

I drop my "hope for the future" story into the guidance councillor's box outside his office with a bit of sarcasm. The future may not be bright, but at least I can laugh.

III

There is a growing sense of uncertainty in the world. Bill Clinton takes over as president in January of 1993 and although he is seen as a new, hipper version of George Bush Senior, he's still part of the old guard.

There's no real change and nobody is feeling optimistic. The shine of a bright future for all has rubbed off and the reality of a rich/poor divide is already setting in. Even at our age.

Eric's Trip keeps busy and productive and contributes a song to an east coast Sub Pop compilation called *Never Mind The Molluscs* and another to a Canadian compilation called *Raw Energy*, with bands from all across the country. This is the first time their music will be available outside of the Maritimes. Their album on Murderecords, *Peter*, is released in April and Sub Pop releases their six-song EP *Songs about Chris* in May. They also put together two more EPs before the year is up, *Trapped in New York* (Summershine Records) and *Warm Girl* (Derivative Records).

In April, they begin work on their first full-length album for Sub Pop. Things are still a bit cold between Rick and Julie and about to get colder. A girl named Tara Landry is emerging as Moncton High's new "it" girl. A short, cute, rocker chick who plays music, she is getting a lot of attention, especially from the jean jacket set, and though a lot of girls were trying to at the time, she had caught Rick's eye. For Rick, this would lead to works of art, hurt feelings, and future muses and music to come.

While they're working on the full-length, Julie finds some writing in Rick's journals. Convinced he is cheating on her, she confronts him. They fight and try to figure it out but things are not quite the same. Around this time, perhaps seeing what the future might hold, Julie starts her own label. Sappy Records is formed to help promote locals and friends who are creating music and who might not be able to reach people on a national or international level. That July, Julie releases her first solo project, *Broken Girl*, and plays a show in Halifax. It sounds like all the things people love about Eric's Trip but toned down and more upbeat, without the heavy distortion.

Rick and Julie continue to work together, no longer a couple but still friends. They try to keep their relationship problems from the rest of the band and continue working on the album. They do some touring near the end of the summer, while the record is being finished.

In a strange and cruel irony, Rick decides he wants to call the new album *Love Tara*. He is now more open about his feelings for Landry and the time he is spending with her. The album is released in November with a picture of Rick and Tara embracing on the cover.

In almost back-and-forth, question-and-answer style lyrics, *Love Tara* is personal, tragic, heartbreaking, and universal. You can feel the young love being lost, the need for growth, and the longing just out of reach. Listening to it now, twenty-plus years later, I'm pulled back to the time, the relationships, the confusion, the anger and the angst. This is perhaps what made the album appealing to kids around the world. The teenage condition is a universal one, not reserved for the youth of Moncton, just young people, period.

Some call this album a masterpiece of low-fi '90s music and I think it has to do with the truth expressed through its simplicity. In a world full of marketing, the next big thing, and overproduced everything, this was a band with no other intention than to simply express art and the human condition. Kids were simply looking for truth and the first place they looked was music.

Love Tara is released to critical success and begins selling well in Canada and the US. It is not a mainstream sound, so it has limited reach beyond college radio and music people in the know. But the band, now hometown heroes, has a cult following in Moncton and the Maritimes. The success of *Love Tara* also helps spawn the Halifax Pop Explosion, a two-week indie music festival. Started by Peter Rowan and legendary Halifax promoter Greg Clark, with its first iteration in September 1993, it was strongly supported by Sub Pop, who provided some of the early bands to help get the festival off the ground. It was the biggest thing going in the early '90s, giving east coast bands a legitimate place to showcase their music. It also helped provide a launching pad for a sound to emerge and spread out across the country. It has seen many ups and downs over the years, including name changes and one year, in 2000, when organizers couldn't get funding or volunteers to get the event off the ground. But there's no question it has made its mark and secured its place establishing Halifax and the east coast as a solid music city, welcoming bands like Arcade Fire, Peaches, and Broken Social Scene, and even drawing influential New York writers like Legs McNeil to early festivals, creating a buzz long before it was cool. This camaraderie between bands would become a staple of the scene and part of what made things work in the Maritimes at this time. Bands helping bands, setting up showcases and festivals and labels like Sappy, recording others to help move them forward.

Being signed to Sub Pop wasn't a huge deal to the members of Eric's Trip. They weren't really looking for fame or attention; they just wanted to continue making art and music. But the ripple effects in their home city were obvious. Like the effects The Clash and The Ramones had on the youth of the '70s, Eric's Trip spawned a new generation of kids, who saw them as pioneers; they were breaking down barriers, helping others pick up instruments of their own. The "if they can do it, we can do it" attitude was in full swing and the pawn shops were full of three-quarter-length-sleeve-wearing teens buying second-hand guitars, duct taping their straps and lead cords. The evolution of being comfortable with who we were and where we were from had begun to wash over us. Eric's Trip helped us realize it was our differences that made us unique.

III

The year ends with what had become a yearly tradition for Eric's Trip: a Christmas show at one of the bars downtown with The Monoxides and Purple Knight. It would remain a Moncton tradition for many years. People home for the holidays, university students, and crowds getting together sharing old stories. Locals are proud of the sound happening around them, and they're excited about the possibilities and the attention the area is getting.

In the New Year Eric's Trip tours across Ontario and Quebec to enthusiastic crowds. Their fan base is growing, and shows are starting to sell out. Considering everything that's happened between Rick and Julie, the band is functioning pretty well. Rick and Chris move into an apartment in downtown Moncton and it becomes a recording studio, flophouse, and drug den. The two begin experimenting with weed and hash and find the process only increases their creativity and productivity. Early that year, 1994, Eric's Trip records another EP, called *The Gordon Street Haunting*. Named for the street where Rick and Chris's downtown apartment is located, the album is definitely more psychedelic, introverted, and far from mainstream. If there was ever a conscious decision by the band to push back with their music, this EP and era would be it.

As Rick's relationship changes with Julie, so does his motivation and connection to her as his muse. He begins spending more and more time with Tara Landry, who has started calling herself Tara S'Appart, and he teaches her how to play bass, the same way he did with Julie only a few years before. With fresh inspiration, he forms a new band with Tara, called Elevator to Hell.

Julie is now distancing herself from the Gordon Street apartment, the drugs, and Rick's new infatuation. She begins spending more time in Ontario with Moncton friends and fellow musicians. She has her own ideas of what the future holds and although she is excited about the success of Eric's Trip, she is not sure where it's all going. Mark Gaudet is now playing drums with Rick and Tara in the Elevator formation and Chris Thompson is working on his own solo project, Moonsocket.

At this time, Rick and Chris start writing the next Eric's Trip album, *Forever Again*. The apartment provides Rick the opportunity to jam and write constantly and work out new music for both of his bands. The separation and new configuration of lovers hasn't affected Eric's Trip directly and the band plans to meet and begin recording in the spring. Everyone is hoping the dynamic will be the same when Julie returns from Ontario. Only then she calls Rick and tells him she's pregnant. Even though he's now dating Tara and knows he had hurt Julie, Rick is devastated by the news. Things would never be the same.

Eric's Trip gets together in May to record. Songs are personal, raw but catchy. Everything the band members are going through is laid out in the song lyrics. Rick is trying to make sense of what has happened; so is the rest of the band. They are still trying to find their sound and moving toward a mix of folky, punk psychedelia. The band is more mature by nature, especially from the ups and downs of the last few years. Mark, who's hanging around a lot jamming with Elevator, and Chris feel more involved, since the album was conceived and recorded at the downtown apartment. Julie feels a bit distant from the others.

Around this time, Eric's Trip and Sloan record each other's songs for a local Halifax 7-inch, *Stove/Smother/Laying Blame*. It is released to support Dalhousie University's radio station, CKDU-FM, which, with a mandate to play new, underground, unheard bands, and no commercial music, is instrumental to up and coming bands. Sloan then contributes their version of Eric's Trip's "Stove/Smother" to a rarities, B-sides CD released by DGC. The album gets a lot of attention.

Eric's Trip's second full-length for Sub Pop, *Forever Again*, breaks down barriers with its smoother tones and more accessible sound when it's released in September 1994. The band also releases its second music video—this one with a bit of a budget and some outside help, unlike their first, self-released video, "My Room"—for the song "ViewMaster." Filmed in and around Moncton by a friend of the band, it gets regular rotation on MuchMusic, increasing the band's already rising popularity. More people begin to appreciate what some of us have already: the subtle art of independent music without expectations.

Despite the band's increasing success, Mark gets the feeling things are not going to last. He sees what others are ignoring or trying to avoid. Chris begins writing songs and focusing a bit more on Moonsocket. Elevator has put together an album. Everyone is making things work and Eric's Trip is the strongest it has ever been musically, but there may not have been enough hills to climb or battles to conquer. They are now a signed band with a professional music video; things are working well and the shine of Rick's original muse has rubbed off. Like a lot of people who get what they want, the chase is often much more exciting than the catch.

Rick and the rest of the band wouldn't be the first people from Moncton or any small town to spend their whole lives dreaming and working hard to reach their goals. They also wouldn't be the first or last to be unsatisfied, even disappointed, when they achieved them. When you grow up in an area without any expectations, you learn not to set your goals too high. For those who work hard and get to the places they never expected, being forced to set new goals can be confusing and disheartening. For Rick, who was still in love with Julie when he got the call from her in Ontario, letting him know she was pregnant with her new boyfriend's child, it became hard to see his little intimate basement band the same way.

Rick starts to put more effort into Elevator and in December 1994 decides to submit a demo to Sub Pop to see if they're interested. They are, and release it the following February. Simply called *Elevator to Hell*, the album has a harder edge and heavier distortion—if that's possible—with more of a hook. It's stoner rock at its finest with lots of experimental sounds. The release does not help tensions in Eric's Trip, and gives Rick even more reason to distance himself from Julie. Age, ego, and pain contribute to a lack of communication between the rest of the band and with Julie now married to artist and childhood friend Jon Claytor, the band's touring schedule is limited. Chris, Rick, and Mark do a few interviews and acoustic shows to promote *Forever Again* and rumours begin to spread the end is near. Julie is not seen in Eric's Trip, Rick has a new band (Elevator) with a new girl, Tara Landry, on bass, and Eric's Trip is not touring. Everyone is denying breakup talk when asked, but nobody is surprised when it finally happens a year later.

Strange as Eric's Trip has been, Elevator to Hell releases its next 7-inch, *Forward to Snow*, on Julie's label, Sappy records, in April of 1995. Just as things are winding down and the band is entering the last phase of its original incarnation, Rick, Chris, Mark, and Julie get the biggest opportunity of their professional lives, from an unexpected source. It could help them move forward or drive them headlong into the ground.

7

GOING SOLO

Things have changed since the early days, playing music in Chris Thompson's parents' basement. Eric's Trip is signed with a major label in the US, and has expectations to follow up its now successful independent masterpiece, *Love Tara*. And the raw energy, emotion, and love that fuelled the band in the beginning is starting to fizzle, as Rick and Julie speak less and less.

Bands, like any relationship, evolve. Sometimes they grow together and the rest of us benefit from the pain and awkwardness of their youth and early adulthood; they put that energy into words and music and create art everyone relates to. Some bands grow with their audiences, over a generation or two. We watch as they shed their skins and reinvent themselves as a way to deal with the changes all around them. There is a reason only a few bands survive these turbulent years.

Like a family or marriage, it's tough. When you put four people together, everything is up for debate: artistic differences, points of view, touring, politics—even what to have for lunch. Trying to make decisions, especially creative ones, can get messy. Put young people together and you add a new component to the mix. Throw in love, ego, jealousy, hurt feelings, and a touch of fame, well.

On the outside, Eric's Trip continues to develop a strong and loyal fan base since the wider release of their Sub Pop albums, and one of their biggest supporters is The Tragically Hip's frontman, Gordon Downie. In 1993 the Hip starts a travelling summer festival called Another Roadside Attraction, aimed at promoting smaller, lesser-known bands from across the country. Eric's Trip accepts an invite to play a series of shows in the summer of 1995. Thousands of fans fill the racetracks, fields, and outdoor concert sites to see a wide variety of music they might not have known, bands like Blues Traveler, Matthew Sweet, The Rheostatics and Ziggy Marley. Playing to the biggest crowds of their career, Eric's Trip branches out to even more people who might not have found them in the obscure sections of record stores, or on the underground radio stations where they are now getting heavy rotation.

But the new attention and big shows can't solve the issues creating a wedge in the band. The huge cost of keeping tour buses on the road eats up all the cash they're making. After six years of working hard, making music, touring, and turmoil, the band is tired, demoralized, living hand to mouth, and not seeing much of a future together. Even though their sound is growing and they are keeping ahead of the curve with a new heavy but catchy version of where they started, it isn't enough to hold the band together.

In May of 1996, the Hip releases the five-times-platinum-selling album, *Trouble at the Henhouse*, with the song "Put it Off." In this haunting self reflection, Downie immortalizes the band with lyrics that include a mention of the album Love Tara, and the name of the band, bringing Eric's Trip to the consciousness of the Canadian mainstream. The Hip are as big as it gets in Canada and people all of sudden know the album *Love Tara*. They are singing it in their cars, on patios, and at cottages.

Everybody in Moncton thinks for sure Eric's Trip is going to be the biggest band on the planet after this. There is no bigger band in the country at this time than The Tragically Hip and no voice stronger than Gordon Downie's. He's always sung about the history and culture of our country and informed us of our oral heritage, laid over classic-rock drums, whining guitars, and a steady bass beat.

Even though this should have been the biggest boost to their career, Eric's Trip is struggling. Julie is a new mom and not interested in being on the road. Things are better with Rick, though he is still on a serious drug experimentation binge. Not a drinker or drugger in high school, he's making up for lost time at the Gordon Street apartment, finding inspiration in mind-altering states. He and Tara are now talking about getting married.

Julie releases another solo album under her Sappy Records label and calls it *Nora*. She is starting to take the Broken Girl idea more seriously, as she must be able to see the inevitable arc the band is taking. Rick begins work on tunes that appear on two compilations, Sonic Unyon's *...Not If I Smell You First!* and *Skookum Chief Powered Teenage Zit Rock Angst* by Vancouver journalist Nardwuar the Human Serviette, but things are coming to an end. All four members of the band are now working solo: Rick and Mark with Elevator, Chris with Moonsocket, and Julie with Broken Girl. Eric's Trip opened up a creative flow and the faucet is starting to unload. Fuelling each other's motivation to make music, all four of the band members are moving further away from the core of what brought them together. Thinking less and less of their music lives as linear, they branch out in many different sounds, styles, and directions.

From the outside looking in, people wonder what's in store for Eric's Trip. The band is at the height of its popularity. Big shows, mass distribution, tours outside the country, and recognition as the coolest band around. We can't help but wonder why all the talk, the drama, the breakup rumours. People are also interested in how this group found themselves and where this Moncton wave originated from. A place so far off the map, with no previous attention and few prospects, is now top of mind for music fans all over the world.

III

Eric's Trip has new songs ready to go and begins talking about their next album, *Purple Blue*, in September of 1995. Sub Pop wants the band to record in a studio to increase their chances of a cleaner, more widespread sound. They've also arranged for Boston-based Bob Weston, who had worked on a ton of punk and underground records in the US and Canada, including Eric's Trip's *Love Tara* and Nirvana's *In Utero*, to come to Moncton to engineer.

The band will have a few obligations to support the album but everybody is becoming consumed with their solo work and moving away from Eric's Trip. They record together in a studio for the first time, everyone playing live off the floor. This is a departure for a band used to recording parts separately, in basements, and piecing them together after the fact.

That October, in the middle of putting the new album together, Rick and Tara get married. The band works hard to keep the album pure, despite their new professional distractions, keeping the edge on the sound, with low tones and grumble. The rhythm section is tighter than ever, harder-hitting with more precise, deliberate strikes to keep the motor of the songs moving forward. But the guitars are more welcoming with an aim to make the songs less full and more airy. There is no lack of dreamy stoner rock here but the wall of distortion has come down. This is a heavy album with waves of pop influences, much like future Elevator to Hell albums would produce. Moncton's Top 40 radio station influences would start to show their heads here. And this would not be a bad thing for musicians looking to grow.

Eric's Trip's songs now have a new sound, the evolution of six years together and everyone's experimentation in their separate projects. The album finishes very strong and everyone in the band is happy with how it turns out. It is the most approachable blend of hard and soft, catchy and underground, individual and collaborative the four of them has ever produced. As a band, they have never sounded better; personally, they all knew this would be their last album as Eric's Trip.

Purple Blue is released on January 16, 1996, with plans for a US tour. There is no doubt anymore this will be the band's last album; they've decided after the tour they will play their last show. Everything the band stood for in the beginning is now starting to break apart. There is nothing left to fight for or against and everybody knows it. Side projects are now more important and Eric's Trip has led everyone to this point.

The pressure of being in a band, signed to a label, with a sound becoming more mainstream all around you, had to be putting constraints on all of them, whether they knew it or not. Hearing music coming out of the west and feeling the expectations from fans to join in and sound the same because it's becoming more accepted brought the band to a place not everyone had agreed to go in the beginning. Rick begins adding "They're trying to sell me" to thought bubbles of Eric's Trip shirts. He is clearly not happy with where things are going.

Eric's Trip's new sound is more progressive and likeable and miles ahead of what most bands of the time are doing, but it is also becoming a bit more mainstream. Not radio-mainstream, but away from the music that would challenge fiends, the same way connoisseurs know great movies, art, cheese, or wine. This begins to push each member of the band in their own musical direction.

For Chris, who is feeling better about leading his own band, Moonsocket, writing his own songs, and taking things in a more experimental direction, it is always going to be lo-fi, experimental, do-it-yourself, stoner rock.

Rick and Mark keep pushing the acid-rock sounds they started with Elevator to Hell, eventually morphing to Elevator through Hell, then to just Elevator (they were worried about taking the Elevator straight to the worst place imaginable). Their music is a combination of two things: a fresh muse for Rick, and Mark's not wanting to let go of having a band about friends and good times. Their sound evolves into a heavier, deeper groove. Rick's voice comes out of its shell and plays a more prominent role in how the band sounds and presents itself. Tara proves to be a strong bass player with foot-tapping riffs and Mark keeps the beat chugging along with his freight-train drumming. Still very cool, very weird, and noisy, the band keeps alive the traditions Eric's Trip started.

Despite it all, Julie is developing her voice as an artist and musician with her own sensibilities. Her music is coming together and she is making connections with other locals. Her first few albums show incredible promise as a mix between brokenhearted love songs and singer-songwriter power. In between two worlds, she is a little hesitant to completely pull away from the band that gave birth to her identity as an artist.

Still, with each song, each album, and every passing moment, Julie's music gets stronger and gives her the confidence to move beyond the tough years that helped her grow. No longer needing the security of the band, she feels it is time to take her music and life in a new direction, for good. It's around this time she begins working with Sub Pop; they release her solo album *Broken Girl* in April 1996.

Rick is still hitting the drugs hard. Like most young men in Moncton at the time, he is lost in isolation without huge purpose. Even those with talent, vision, and ambition, and despite the rock and roll prospects, life still felt stagnant for kids growing up in the Maritimes. This wall of low self-esteem holding everyone back was like a curtain nobody could see beyond. First, no one had really gone beyond Moncton with music, so there was no precedent for doing so. Second, none of us really believed anyone could do it. We didn't think the rest of the country or the world would take us seriously. And this didn't just apply to music; it applied to everything.

Love Tara begins making its way onto Top Canadian Albums of All Time lists and people start to see how the world outside of Moncton viewed their music. There are still break-up rumours, but there always were. Julie is now friends with Tara, who, now married to Rick for a few months, is seen hanging out with Eric's Trip, in videos, at parties, and at shows. Everyone thinks the whole Rick, Julie, and Tara thing is in the past and the bands are gaining momentum. Eric's Trip, Elevator, and the solo projects are opening for each other, attracting crowds, and creating a scene within the scene. It's like the new guard has come in and taken over, creating venues with their friends and loads of people to follow. They had defied everything expected of them. Making music in their basements, selling tapes out of a small independent record shop, getting regional and national attention without even trying, and turning down a contract from one of the biggest indie labels until it was more favourable on their terms.

Their hometown ease and inexperience, largely what attracted fans in the first place, eventually becomes a part of Eric's Trip's undoing. So does Rick's daily binging on weed, hash, and acid. As the band begins to prepare for what would be its last tour through the US and Canada, members are excited about the venues and cities they plan to play while on the road: Boston, New York, Washington, D.C. All the things they ever dreamed of doing as a band, going on a real tour, being on a real label, not having to work real jobs, being with friends, making music they wanted to make: it's all coming true. Some of the shows even start selling out in advance; others the day of.

In an interview with CBC three years earlier, Rick, Mark and Julie had spoken about life on the road.

"When we go out on the road now, or whatever, it's still fun," Rick said to the *Ear to the Ground* host.

"Yeah, but once it starts to be a habit or once it's starts to be really uncomfortable—if we wanna, like, kill each other or anything like that—I think that it would be no more fun," Julie said, still hoping at this point to tour more.

"I think we can all agree that we don't want to go out for too long," said Rick, speaking for the band. "We'd rather be here in Moncton, just in our basements, sleeping and recording songs." Rick seemed quite sure of this at the time, three years before the band would break up.

"Julie is the little, kinda guardian angel to the band," Mark later added. "It seems that she can hold us together, that she's a good luck charm.

I don't know if things would've happened quite as good without Julie to tell you the truth. I know Rick's so talented for the songs and everything but I just have this feeling as a team they're almost stronger and all that. And I hope they don't ever break up," he added in an almost prophetic statement.

Anxiety starts to build as the band enters the US, playing small venues leading to bigger shows in Massachusetts and New York. Shows go well, but the band is living on a small per diem and everyone starts to question where the cash is going from all the ticket sales. This would be a contentious issue for band members, who claim they never saw a dollar from Sub Pop—not even twenty-plus years later with re-releases of their albums. Driving into and out of some of the biggest urban centres, especially late at night, with little money put a lot of stress on four young people who had barely been out of Moncton.

After only a handful of shows, Rick, who hadn't wanted to leave on tour in the first place, starts to have second thoughts. He's not happy, and with a combination of homesickness, withdrawal, and frustration over the band's commitments, he plots leaving the tour and the band. The reality of what's happened over the past six years is now settling in, and being stuck in a van to think about it is too much. Rick is restless and by the time they get to New York, he tells everyone he's leaving and going home. The freedom of being in a band with your girlfriend, writing songs about feelings and trying to express them in the most original, raw, and truthful way, was gone. For Rick, being on the road to support someone else's record and living off of pennies had taken the art out of everything and went against the very reason the band had started in the beginning.

Julie, Mark, and Chris are not happy; they do not want to abandon the tour and their commitment to Sub Pop. Especially when fans are showing up to gigs, night after night. But Rick is done. It becomes clear whose band it really is when nobody can talk Rick out of his decision. The band drives back home, quietly, understanding it's over. The same band that had come so far, who had re-defined a sound and made people pay attention, is done, just like that.

RICK DURING ERIC'S TRIP'S FIRST SHOW, APRIL 22 (EARTH DAY), 1991, AT MONCTON'S CITY HALL.

RICK AND JULIE DURING ERIC'S TRIP'S FIRST SHOW, APRIL 22 (EARTH DAY), 1991, AT MONCTON'S CITY HALL.

FULL BAND, INCLUDING ED VAUGHAN ON DRUMS, AT THE WAREHOUSE PUB, JULY 13, 1991.

RICK AND CHRIS AT THE WAREHOUSE PUB, JULY 13, 1991, FEATURING ORIGINAL DRUMMER, ED VAUGHAN.

ERIC'S TRIP AT LE KACHO, FEBRUARY 10, 1992. MARK'S FIRST SHOW WITH THE BAND. WE WERE SURPRISED THAT MARK, OUR OLDER LOCAL PUNK CULT HERO, JOINED THIS YOUNG, ALTERNATIVE BAND THAT HAD BIGGER ASIPRATIONS THAN MOST. NOTICE MARK USING TWO BASS DRUMS.

GROUP SHOT OF ERIC'S TRIP AT LE KACHO, FEBRUARY 10, 1992. MARK'S FIRST SHOW.

RICK WHITE AT LE KACHO, FEBRUARY 10, 1992. MARK'S FIRST SHOW WITH ERIC'S TRIP.

ERIC'S TRIP AT THE BLACK ROSE, MONCTON, MARCH 5, 1992.

MARK GAUDET BEHIND THE DRUMS FOR AN ERIC'S TRIP SHOW AT THE BLACK ROSE, MONCTON, APRIL 15, 1992.

ERIC'S TRIP PERFORMING AT SCREAMER'S IN MONCTON, OPENING FOR REDD KROSS, SEPTEMBER 28, 1993.

REDD KROSS, SEPTEMBER 28, 1993, AT SCREAMER'S BAR IN MONCTON. THE BAND WORE MATCHING ERIC'S TRIP SHIRTS ON STAGE.

RICK AND JULIE AT ROOM 201 RECORDS IN MONCTON SOMETIME IN 1993, JUST AFTER *SONGS ABOUT CHRIS* WAS RELEASED. THEY WERE REGULARS. THEY WOULD BRING THEIR TAPES, RECORDS, AND T-SHIRTS IN ON CONSIGNMENT, HANG OUT, AND TALK MUSIC.

THIS ERIC'S TRIP DISPLAY STAND FROM SAM THE RECORD MAN NOW LIVES IN MARK GAUDET'S JAM ROOM. PHOTO TAKEN IN FEBRUARY 2016.

JULIE AND RICK AT ERIC'S TRIP'S LAST SHOW, JUNE 16, 1996, AT MONCTON'S MACNAUGHTON SCIENCE AND TECHNOLOGY CENTRE.

CHRIS AND JULIE DURING ERIC'S TRIP'S LAST SHOW, JUNE 16, 1996, AT MONCTON'S MACNAUGHTON SCIENCE AND TECHNOLOGY CENTRE. THEY HAD DONE SO MUCH AS A BAND IN SIX YEARS; NOW IT WAS TIME TO CLOSE THE BOOK.

CHRIS KNEELING WITH HIS GUITAR DURING ERIC'S TRIP'S FAREWELL SHOW AT THE MACNAUGHTON SCIENCE AND TECHNOLOGY CENTRE, JUNE 16, 1996.

Some say they'd seen it all coming for a long time; others are shocked at the news.

Eric's Trip announces their final show will take place at the MacNaughton Science and Technology Centre in June, where their friends Sloan will join them for a near-sold-out show of over eight hundred people. Andrew Campbell, the teacher responsible for creating the recording studio, sound booth, and jam space where Rick White borrowed his first 4-tracks to record the original Eric's Trip cassettes, helps organize the show. After helping hundreds of other kids learn the fundamentals of sound mixing, recording, tuning, and editing, as well as song writing, Campbell is just trying to make sure nobody gets hurt and the high-school cafeteria doesn't get destroyed with more and more kids lining up at the door, trying to get in.

MuchMusic shows up with cameras and interviews Rick and Mark about the final show, the end of an era. Rick seems anxious to get it over with, while Mark is quite nostalgic, thanking MuchEast for all their support and telling them to look forward to more Eric's Trip releases in the future (they still had music recorded, which they planned to release), as well as talking about the members' other bands and how there is more to come from them. Rick mentions Elevator to Hell and how they are working on a new album and plan to have a new video in the fall. Mark is excited, and you can tell they're both happy to be home, close to friends and familiar surroundings.

When Ken Kelley from The Monoxides motions for Mark and Rick to head to the stage, the interview comes to an end. "I don't know what to say," says Mike Campbell, the VJ from MuchEast. "I feel kind of sad." Rick and Mark wave to the camera and walk away.

Sloan has just played, having driven up from Halifax. The crowd is wired from their performance. It's hot, dark, and crowded on the flat cement floor of the open cafeteria, where barricades separate the band. Security is working overtime trying to keep everyone settled and safe as hundreds of fans push forward; they're forced to remove kids who were being crushed, one at a time. Every musician, skateboarder, and outcast in the city is here. Six long years of friends, fans, and figuring out how the band got so popular.

The night ends with people spreading out all over the high-school parking lot. Kids walking down the long road, out onto the busy street. Some hang around the football field, others dip into the park, everyone talking about the power, energy, and style of our music scene. For a place once concerned with being nowhere, being known for nothing, we all of a sudden felt a surge of cool. Those walking out of the building were no longer poseurs, trying to copy what was going on around them; they were trendsetters. We were a part of the scene, instead of simply hearing about it.

Eric's Trip had made a huge impression on all those around them, especially those right here in their hometown. You could see it in the way people dressed, walked, and talked on the night of their final show. Jean jackets and sneakers, T-shirts and long hair, these were now the norm among those who made it their life's work not to ever wear a tie. They gave permission to those who thought they could never do anything other than what their parents had done—working at plants or in retail, in factories or on farms—and let them dream a little wider.

Nobody was getting rich making music. Eric's Trip had not made any money from touring, royalties or otherwise, but that wasn't the point. They were the first real band in Moncton to show others you could make music because you wanted to, and you could do it on your own terms.

III

In the summer of 1996, as the members of Eric's Trip went their separate ways, the rest of the thousand or so people who saw them that night walked away with something important. It was the collective understanding the band did not put into their songs but had passed on in their six-year journey from their first cassette to their last official album. The same message bands the members of Eric's Trip grew up listening to passed on to them: it can be done, and you don't need anyone's permission to do it, inspiring them to pick up instruments and create their own songs. Nothing they did on stage that night was beyond a little ambition and a little hard work. They encouraged everyone to get out of their own way and find their own talent.

There was still much more to come for the members, without Eric's Trip.

8

THE SLOW DESCENT

alf the band has moved on, leaving Rick and Mark in Moncton to keep Elevator to Hell blossoming and playing shows in the area. They do a few shows with Sloan around this time and Sub Pop releases Elevator's *Parts 1-3* album in August 1996. They're continuing on where Eric's Trip left off, with Tara on bass, an evolved sound grounded in their artistic roots, still pushing to find creative perfection. Prolific as ever, they also release a 7-inch called *Backwards May* in September on Julie's Sappy outfit.

Not to be outdone, Chris Thompson releases another Moonsocket album, *The Best Thing*, around this time, making the leap from former band member to true solo artist. Worried about what the future held, he had pushed on, the security of being in a band and contributing to the collective giving him some confidence. Putting music out there is scary at the best of times, but with no band to fall back on, it made the journey to continue with music even harder.

Julie is now travelling between Ontario, Montreal, and Sackville, New Brunswick. She is raising a son, focusing on Sappy Records, and making music, working hard on her solo work. The next year Sub Pop releases her album *Loneliest in the Morning*, and Sappy releases a compilation of Eric's Trip material, *Long Days Ride 'Till Tomorrow*. Never a dull moment, Julie also tours with former Underdogs member Mike Feuerstack's band Wooden Stars, a Sappy artist, in the fall.

Not concerned with making money, Rick continues to create music on his own terms. Fuelled by drugs and friends he keeps pushing the possibilities of independent music. Never settling for anything safe, *Parts 1-3* is hard to describe and even harder to categorize. Like a mosaic of sound, it's grungy garage rock one minute and '60s pop the next. Far ahead of its time, it only appeals to those looking for the most obscure underground rock. There is a sense that Rick is deliberately trying to sabotage his own work. In an almost remorseful tone, his lyrics refer to the women he's lost and mistakes he's made. It feels more and more like he's pushing the world away. Elevator tours, but realizes the old fans are not quite as open to the new arrangement.

The band starts working on its next album, *Eerieconsiliation*, recording in February 1997. It starts out heavy and has a strong Eric's Trip vibe. The rest of the album is a mix of soft and hard with Mark adding vocals halfway through. A hit with loyal fans, it sends the band further away from its core Eric's Trip audience and alienates them completely from everyone else. Rick is starting to get exactly what he wanted: a respected, obscure band, known only to collectors, musicians, and true fans.

Small pressings of Elevator's albums make them hard to come by for fans outside New Brunswick. The internet helps the band's myth and legend grow, and members relish in their geographic obscurity.

They're now free to work on music and hide away as those outside the area wonder what they're up to next. Moncton provides a great place to live cheap and create. The comfort and safety of it all keeps Rick's anxiety in check and gives him the motivation to write songs. and work on his next project.

Around this time, Rick meets Dallas Good of the Canadian alt-country band The Sadies. In a lot of ways, they are the same person: old '60s and '70s acid rock and vinyl fans; long-haired guitar players with a DIY sensibility. They had a lot to talk about. Both were determined to make the music they wanted to, music that didn't necessarily fit any mould or satisfy the needs of mainstream audiences. The Sadies have a long pedigree in Canadian music. Dallas and Travis Good are the sons of Margaret and Bruce Good, nephews of Brian and Larry Good, who were a part of a Canadian bluegrass country outfit called The Good Brothers, reaching back to the early '70s scene. Dallas would eventually become a collaborator with Rick in Elevator to Hell, playing guitar and helping to add depth to the sound.

Always working on something, Rick puts together a small, obscure art film called *The Such*, using Moncton as the backdrop. It's shown at a few galleries in the area, where people get a better sense of where Rick's mind is at the moment, and the soundtrack is released on Murderecords. (Today, both the film and soundtrack are very hard to find.)

Always following his mantra of creating art and putting it out there, Rick and Tara use their Elevator shows to bring back an old project even more obscure than the others. Perplexis started in the early '90s and was basically a collection of trippy sounds made with Casio keyboards. It went back to the original, minimalist idea of punk rock: trying to get something from nothing (or at least very little). It usually starts with musicians who have music and melodies in their heads before they can play their instruments, who start trying to get the sounds out anyway they can. Like tapping your foot or strumming with one finger on a guitar, these sounds can be made and improvised to create something that is music, before it's music. Rick recorded these incarnations and gave them numbers: Perplexis #1, #2 etc.... He only ever sold one recording, #7, about one hundred copies. It is strange and different and all things you would expect from musicians pushing the limits of their own creativity.

Julie is also keeping busy. In August 1998 she releases a book of photographs called *The Longest Winter*. She also starts playing more with Sappy recording artist and longtime friend Mike Feuerstack, and during a tour with Wooden Stars, they back up Doiron on a couple of songs. It sounds great and the two decide to record an album that December called *Julie Doiron and the Wooden Stars*. They record another the following September, called *Will You Still Love Me*, and the two are well received.

In a bit of a surprise, *Julie Doiron and the Wooden Stars* wins the 2000 Juno Award for Alternative Album of the Year. The band that came together by accident, whose members Julie (who was happy being solo) thought were too different to play together, ended up creating something stronger than their collective parts. Gordon Downie, a fan of Doiron's since her days in Eric's Trip, asks her to contribute vocals for the new Tragically Hip album, *Music @ Work* (2000), and she spends a day in the studio singing and playing piano. (She would later work on Downie's solo albums, *Coke Machine Glow* [2001] and *The Battle of the Nudes* [2003].) Soon after, Doiron begins work on a Francophone album called *Désormais,* which she releases in August of 2001.

As for Elevator to Hell, between name changes and new releases on different labels, people start to get confused about who the band is and what they're all about. On posters, they appear as ELEVATOR TO HELL one week, ELEVATOR THROUGH HELL the next. The band doesn't change, and neither does the music. The trip is getting weird and not everybody gets it.

Starting to go by Elevator, the band begins working on its next album, *Eerieconsiliation*, recording in February 1997. The band continues to put out music on compilations and starts work on their final album for Sub Pop, *Vague Premonition*, releasing it in April 1999. Rick then puts together a live Elevator album and releases it under his own label, Great Beyond, that June. Dallas Good now officially joins the band and starts to tour with Rick, Tara, and Mark. They put together *A Taste of Complete Perspective* and release it in September 2000. Feeling the long-term effects of his drug abuse, and with married life proving tough, Rick decides to move the band to Toronto.

But Rick has a hard time functioning and retreats further inward. He plays drums in a cover band with Dallas and his brother, but music is not paying the bills and the artist life is putting huge strains on his and Tara's relationship. With the couple now broke and struggling, Tara takes a job cleaning in Toronto.

At this time, Rick makes a random call to Julie, sparking a conversation about why Eric's Trip broke up and all the loose ends Rick felt guilty about. Leaving the 1996 tour midway and breaking up the band had left him feeling bad about how it all ended. A lot had happened since then and, feeling particularly vulnerable, they decide to book some reunion shows.

Eric's Trip reunites in the summer of 2001 for the hello again/goodbye forever tour. The shows during the three-week, cross-Canada tour are a hit and the band very briefly discusses doing other shows, but nothing ever materializes. Everybody is now into their own thing. Side projects have turned into full-time gigs and Eric's Trip is no longer a priority for anyone. The excitement is gone and nobody likes the novelty of playing to satisfy nostalgia. Even Mark, who thought the band had more left to create, could see the writing on the wall. "I knew it wasn't going to work out," he says from his record room in 2015.

Julie returns to Sackville more regularly and begins playing with a new group of musicians. They decide to put a band together, and Shotgun & Jaybird, made up of Fred Squire, Jim Kilpatrick, and Paul Henderson at the time, start backing Julie on some of her solo shows. Julie starts playing bass again for the first time since Eric's Trip. The band is more rock-inspired and she is having fun jamming with no pressure; once again, it's just four people getting together and making music.

For her next solo album, Doiron wants to put a band together to get the same jam feel she's experiencing with her new friends in Sackville. She calls Rick to ask if he'll help her. She thinks the band should be Rick, Chris, and Mark Gaudet. They all agree. They record the album in Rick's old schoolhouse studio. He and Tara have broken up and he's living in a rural area outside of Toronto. Around this time, Julie's marriage dissolves and the original members of Eric's Trip find themselves back recording drum and guitar parts for Julie's new album, *Woke Myself Up* (2007).

It's around this time that Julie decides to revive Sappy Records. It had not gotten much attention over the last few years, with starts and stops when everyone got too busy. She decides to relaunch the label with a big end-of-summer kickoff, and in August 2006 SappyFest is created. It is the beginning of New Brunswick's best-known independent music festival. Original for many reasons, and homegrown from the beginning, the independent arts and music festival would grow with the work of volunteers, musicians, and the town of Sackville all lending a hand. Today, it is not uncommon to see headliners and festival founders playing on the main stage or selling tickets in between shows. Bands are billeted in houses around town, costs are shared, security becomes a communal responsibility, and everybody pitches in to make it happen every year.

That first year, Julie and Rick both play shows, as do Chris's Moonsocket and Mark's Purple Knight and The Robins. And with everyone all in one place, Eric's Trip decides to headline the event to help ensure the whole thing goes off. They would continue to headline the festival for the next three years, until 2009.

Woke Myself Up is released in January of 2007 and is considered by many to be Doiron's strongest work. Fans of the indie set are happy to get the next best thing to an Eric's Trip album, and the raw lyrics and content are even more interesting as everyone learns about the band's personal turmoil. After receiving a Polaris Prize nomination, the album's profile increases on underground and indie radio.

Rick White releases a couple of solo albums, *The Rick White Album* and *Memoreaper*. He calls the latter "[one of] my favourite created documents of life." Recorded in his own studio, playing all the instruments himself, the album is a self-described rebirth. After his breakup with Tara, he returned home to live in his parents' basement for the winter for a much needed mental and physical break. He wrote songs and symbolically killed off his old life in order to grow into his new one. *The Rick White Album* is dedicated to seven "lovely quilts," the women in his life, including Julie and Tara. The album is a reflection but it also looks ahead. You can hear the fragility in a man trying to feel his way around a world he is isolated from; one he doesn't quite know how he fits into anymore. This is a full departure from where he started from as a teenager. In The Underdogs, he was trying to break down the walls, kick down the doors keeping him isolated. In Eric's Trip and Elevator, he used music to open up the world to our little town. Now he is building those walls back up, all around him.

9

LIFE AFTER ERIC

After releasing *Memoreaper*, Rick is now living happily in the Ontario countryside, able to play, record, and paint whenever he wants. Having spent the past winter recovering in his parent's basement in Moncton, he's now ready to settle into the things that are most important to him. He records a few bands in his home studio for fun. He wants to record that feeling you get seeing a band live, when they're at their best, raw and emotional. Admitting he's not good with money, he pays rent and board with friend and roommate Brian Taylor but has no interest in creating a business from his passions. He wants his art to capture experiences; money and business only takes away from that. He plays a few solo shows in and around Toronto but doesn't tour. In his spare time, he works on an Eric's Trip film of past interviews, live shows, and unseen footage, eventually releasing it online as *Eric's Trip 1990-1996*.

Chris Thompson is working on a new band called The Memories Attack and Doiron follows with a new album, *I Can Wonder What You Did With Your Day*. Mark is busy with his bands, his zine, and growing vinyl collection. He continues to work at Sam's (now Frank's Music), educating Monctonians about music. Elevator continues to be prolific until Rick announces at SappyFest 2009 that the band had broken up. Julie continues to tour and make music in many different forms and by contributing to the work of others. She releases another album in 2012, called *So Many Days*, and spends time in Europe, Japan, and across Canada playing to thousands of fans. One of her songs, "Life of Dreams," is even chosen for a 2014 Apple iPhone 5 commercial. It plays worldwide and exposes her music to an even larger audience. After eighteen years without a new record, Moonsocket releases *Eurydice*, in 2015, exploring grief and sadness.

As far as Eric's Trip, there is no talk of a reunion. Rick doesn't have any interest in revisiting his days in the band. "Eric's Trip's music is for kids to play now," he tells me by email. The battle to grow from those roots was hard won and there are a lot of painful memories. For all four members. Youth can be tough and the growing pains linger. It can be very emotional to pull art out of raw wounds and lay them out in your music; it's not as easy to go back and revisit, even more than twenty years later.

III

The country road leading to Mark Gaudet's house is a beautiful twisty drive lined with trees, churches, small shops, and brooks. Not the type of environment you'd expect to find a hard-hitting, influential punk rock drummer. His hundred-year-old farmhouse looks like the perfect place to film a horror movie: set back from the road, an old barn in the yard, woods and woods and woods for days.

The first thing I see when I walk in the back door is a large piano. The next is a huge Ramones poster. The house is a shrine to music, from tapes to CDs to DVDs. A large fish tank keeps a black cat sitting in a Papasan chair occupied. It purrs at me while I rub its head. I can't help but notice a stack of mail addressed to Mark. Lots of envelopes with a variety of handwriting. Then I see records.

Rumour is Mark only listens to vinyl in the order he buys them. So albums bought today might not get listened to for years. "Yeah," he confirms, "I'm listening to stuff right now from 1999." A pile leans up against his entertainment centre. "Those are some I've bought this year," he says. "I won't get to them for a while."

Mark Gaudet began this tradition in the 1970s when he first started collecting. The problem is, time becomes the enemy: you can only listen to so much music. This has created a backlog in his system, at this point, of more than six years. There are exceptions however. "Some albums jump the rotation," Mark says: "Ritchie Blackmore, Mötley Crue, Celtic Frost."

The house is clean and almost meticulously organized. We sit down to have a beer and talk. Mark is wearing slippers, a cardigan, and jeans. Grey hair covers most of his head. He still looks like the guy on the back cover of *Love Tara*, just a little older. The first thing I notice when talking music with him is his passion. His voice changes, so does his personality; his hands start to move, he gets animated. We start with a little small talk, non-music-related, and we're both stiff, awkward, with not much to say. When he notices the Black Flag T-shirt under my button-up, the conversation goes from good to great: "Black Flag, now there's a band."

We start with punk rock and move to every extreme. Metal, rock, stoner, psychedelic, the Beatles, the Stones, the Monkees: there is nothing about music this guy does not know. And not just in a way people who have been listening to music know bands; the man knows dates of every album and era, who influenced whom and when.

I'm a bit in awe of Mark. There are some people who grow up listening and playing music only to find "real" jobs, reliving their youth by listening to records on weekends—classic rock perhaps—and doing what's best and most important for society—like selling insurance—during the week. Then there's Mark. Started a band in 1974 at age eleven, began working at Sam the Record Man at seventeen, and joined Eric's Trip at twenty-nine. He's the real deal. It's obvious when I look around his home, in the stories he tells me about playing shows across North America. Some for money, some for love, some for pizza or beer. He's played with friends, heroes, and bands he'd never heard of, and he loves it all. No experience in music seems too big or small. It's hard not to notice just how proud Mark is of all the things he's done with music. He's an artist and he doesn't care what the rest of the world does—this is his life.

I ask him about his legendary record collection and he asks if I want to see it. We climb the stairs to the second floor and we're greeted at the top with wall to wall to wall records. I'm a little overwhelmed as I start flipping through the vinyl, trying to make sense of the years of collecting and knowledge and pristine organization, put into this world of rock and roll history.

"Jesus Christ, Mark," I say.

He flips on a light, exposing more tapes, CDs, and records leading down a hall. Everything is labelled with tags and dividers, and albums are covered in plastic. More posters hang on the walls and I feel like this might be the coolest place I've ever been. We talk surf punk bands from California. He tells me how he gets goosebumps when he hears "Bloodstains" by Agent Orange. *Living in Darkness* was one of the first albums I noticed coming up the stairs and one of the first I bought from Mark at Sam's when I was a kid. "It doesn't get much better than that," he says.

We talk European metal and Canadian punk and where they rank in Mark's list of top albums of all time. He calls them "the best albums in the history of the human being." Of course he does. He also has a list by song. From Emerson, Lake and Palmer to Blue Cheer to The Gun Club. The list is diverse, every song chosen for a reason much deeper and profound than you might think. Listening to him talk about these bands, I start to realize how technical, layered, and well thought out the Eric's Trip sound really is. Mark's knowledge of music is so beyond, I get lost in his cross-references of cross-references. Guitar players who started bands who influenced sounds who started revolutions. Kind of like he did.

I could sit and listen all night. But the house is starting to fill up with the smell of something cooking on the stove. I'd met Mark's partner when I first came in. She'd laughed and teased him about listening to music in order and how far behind he was. Now, she was preparing a late-night feast.

We walk into another room and sitting in the middle of the floor is a set of vintage purple-flecked drums, the ones you see Mark playing in Eric's Trip's "ViewMaster" music video. Surrounded by cymbals and well-worn skins, the room is a shrine to Mark's professional life as a drummer. On the back wall stands a life-size, large-eyed, hand-drawn Warm Girl, complete with long, dark hair, courtesy of Rick White. She would be the focal point of the whole room if it weren't covered with tons of similarly interesting artifacts. In the centre of the girl's body, where her hands come together and meet, is a small homemade box with the words ERIC'S TRIP written across it. It has a few 7-inches sitting in it. "It used to be on the wall at Sam's, where we sold our records and CDs," Mark explains.

On the other side of his drums are Sub Pop press photos and copies of the albums Mark has released into the world. Amps, guitars, extra drumsticks, and cords litter the floor. I see now what I hadn't seen before: Mark is not finished with Eric's Trip. He still wants to make music in this vein, still wants to push experimental rock and keep on doing what he's always done. "We still get offers to play and tour with bands," he says. Mark smiles and sits down at the drums. He looks around at all the stuff accumulated in the room: a coloured spiral prop powered by a record player motor used on stage for some of their first shows, Elevator to Hell posters, prints, and originals, as well as some Purple Knight stuff from over the years.

He tells me stories of writing and rehearsing with Eric's Trip in these rooms. The memories still make him smile. The cracked and broken cymbals on his drum kit are reminders of a time he doesn't want to let go of. The room remains an active jam space for Mark's old and new bands. He's always looking for the magic that happens when a few people get together in a room with nothing but their instruments. It starts out noisy, out of tune, off time, and offbeat. Everyone trying to find their place, looking for a riff, a hook, a rhythm or catchy melody. This can go on for minutes, hours, or days. Sometimes jam sessions never produce anything. A bunch of people banging around like a mess. Then, out of a nowhere, everybody gets in tune, on the same page, in the same key. Maybe it only happens for a few seconds or a minute, or maybe a song comes together, but from the first time we all heard music, this is what we're waiting for. I tell Mark about my friends and I jamming and the garage rock, Eric's Trip/Elevator–inspired music we try to make. PJ, Shane, and our friend Melissa, and I hammering it out. I laugh about the frustrations, trying to create a sound that is fun, interesting, and original: the goal of any band young or old. But the moment it all comes together: "Ah, the magic," Mark says. "Isn't it wonderful?"

There are few people in the world like Mark. Committed, disciplined, obsessed with making music about something more. Sitting in his newly renovated listening room, stickers, tapes, and 'zines make my point. There are hundreds and hundreds of tapes and vinyl, perfectly arranged, waiting to be shared. His *Venison Creek* cassettes, part of his long-running 'zine, where he lists the top 10 best albums and songs, sit neatly arranged on a shelf. Demos of every band he's been part of since the '70s are piled along and a sticker stands out: Pond Scum, a band I remember from my skateboarding days in the mid-'80s. He's wearing a pin—Nerve Button, Ray 13's new band. With no interest in money, fame, or punk rock politics, their intentions are pure.

Keeping tradition alive is still important to Mark and his crew. Encouraging the next generation of bands to pick up guitars and create their own sound, something that's important, that has meaning and adds something to the conversation. It takes a long time to come to this realization, years of playing and wanting to achieve all the things young bands look for. Eventually, you realize what's important. "Everything we did with both bands was deliberate," he says, "it had meaning."

A man of tradition, Mark still likes things done a certain way. He takes pride in the meaning behind his decisions and doesn't rush to into anything quickly. Take haircuts for example: He only cuts his hair once a year, in July. He gives himself a near-buzz cut in the middle of the summer and lets it grow the rest of the year. No need to worry about it again until the following summer. He only concerns himself with the important things in life: playing, listening to, and talking about music. In Eric's Trip and Elevator, he and Rick saw the importance in everything from lyrics to band names and artwork. The name Elevator to Hell, for example, was changed because they were worried about the idea of going *to* hell. They thought it over and the idea of going *through* hell made more sense. Passing through would be better. They eventually dropped "Through" and just went with Elevator, making Rick's grandmother happy.

One of Mark's favourite Eric's Trip shirts has their recurring character, who they refer to as Eric, sometimes floating, sometimes long, with big eyes or long hair, meekly crying out, "They're trying to sell me." This is when Mark knew the band was changing and things were going in a different direction. Mark believes timing is everything and when things are done, they're done. "The '90s were our '60s," he says. "It was a celebration, our call to arms."

Mark is still being celebrated. In 2016 he was awarded the Stompin' Tom Honorary East Coast Music Award, which honours musicians and performers who have made an impact on the scene and who are thought to be "unsung heroes." Mark certainly qualifies and the award was well deserved, although he did not attend the ceremony in Sydney, Nova Scotia. He told me he thought about going but there were a lot of things to consider. The travel, the attention, and of course the non-smoking hotel rooms. "You know, it's a whole thing now, you can't smoke anywhere, it's a lot of trouble."

III

Sackville, New Brunswick, is a small, unassuming place. With its art galleries, music venues, and one of the country's best liberal arts universities, it was named 2008's Cultural Capital of Canada. Tucked away on a quiet street, surrounded by coffee shops and an old-school movie theatre, is a storefront with a sign reading PUBLIC HOUSE. There is no sign to let you know it is the home of Thunder & Lightning, a pub that doubles as the Sappyfest offices.

A decade-long non-profit, independent music festival, Sappyfest began as a way to promote bands on Julie Doiron's Sappy record label. It has since risen to become a staple in the east coast alternative scene, attracting bands from all over Canada and beyond. In July of 2011, a band called Shark Attack, scheduled to play under the Sappy tent, had everyone talking. With U2 playing the next night in Moncton with a few opening bands, rumours where spreading about whether somebody from the monster night on Magnetic Hill would make their way to Sackville and surprise the crowd. From the opening drumbeats of "Neighbourhood #2 (Laika)," the crowd of less than a thousand was on its feet. There was no doubt by the amount of bodies on stage and the energy running through the tent on the lower end of Bridge Street: Shark Attack was the Grammy-winning Montreal powerhouse Arcade Fire.

Like all things in the life of Julie Doiron, Thunder & Lightning feels homegrown, kitschy, and completely original. The bar is stocked with a fridge (not a traditional beer cooler) and stuffed animals (as in taxidermy), and there is a dishwasher in the corner, like you might find in your own home. The furniture in the room is a mix of wooden tables and '70s-style brown and orange basement colours, so embarrassing and uncool they fit in perfectly. Old oil paintings mix easily with local art.

I'm here tonight to see Julie and a band from Berlin: Stanley Brinks and Clemence Freschard, a singer-songwriter duo Julie met years ago.

She's been touring with them from Toronto, east. They arrive and put their guitars on the floor while the place fills up with a mix of students, townies, and people of all sorts. Everyone moves around the room, stopping to talk with Julie. She is very friendly, likeable, and approachable.

She grabs her gear and walks through the back door into the bowling alley, where the stage is set up for the show. It's an intimate space, decorated with more art, a deer head, scarves, and mini lights. A small merch area is set up with vinyl. Chairs are scattered in front, creating an informal living room. Bright florescent lights line the lanes of the bowling alley. They're dimmed as the instruments are set up. The stage is low, a couple of feet. It keeps the mood comfortable. This room is full of friends.

The opening band reaches the crowd, which has moved from the front of the house to the back, with their blend of emotional folk and rock. They play up their accents with humour and the crowd relates well to their culturally relevant songs. Connections to our own worldviews keep heads bobbing and feet tapping on the floor of this small room in a small New Brunswick town on a cool September night.

The openers come off stage and mingle. Beers are held up and toasts are made to the performers. The night has a real kitchen-party ambience. Julie comes through the door again, walks on stage, and is joined by the male guitar player from the opening band. They tune a bit, twisting knobs on the ends of their instruments. Julie bends down and adjusts an amp. She twists and pushes buttons, slides her fingers across the strings on her guitar. "We're going to start now," she says. The crowd applauds, happy to see the hometown girl. Everybody is comfortable and laid back, slouched over in jeans and cords, loose sweaters and plaid shirts.

The tempo is quick on the first song, an older jam everybody knows, with fast strumming. Julie is all smiles as she plays along in harmony, jumping into another one, then stopping to talk about where she wrote the lyrics for her next tune. A bit of a vagabond, she spent years moving back and forth between Ontario, Quebec, and

New Brunswick. Toronto was home for a while, then Montreal. Great spots for the artistic life; not so great for cost of living. She once had to play a series of shows in a small Toronto cafe just to pay her rent at the end of the year. Touring and album sales weren't enough to keep the lights on. She's almost quit the music business a few times, most recently in Montreal. Split between writing more commercial albums or maintaining indie credibility, life can be tough for those without a top-ten radio hit and the recognition (and compensation) that comes along with it.

In between songs, Julie is quite chatty and open about her life, her songs, and her process. The crowd listens eagerly. She is a great show-woman, even if she isn't trying to be. She starts and stops, making a mistake on the intro to a song. She just laughs it off and says she hasn't practiced in a long time. It starts again and her voice melts away any thoughts the crowd had moments before. Somewhere between her subtle French accent and her flighty, near-forgetfulness, is a real grassroots talent.

After a dozen or more songs, she asks the crowd if one or two more are okay. She finishes up and joins some friends in the front for a beer. The noise level returns, people turn to face each other, beer glasses ready to be filled up again with dark and amber ales. House music comes on: another Thursday night in a college-town bar. A scene full of music fans, like any other, spilling out into the street, heading back to campus to order pizza.

Julie and I talk a bit about the show, the re-release of *Love Tara*, and tours she has planned for Europe later in the fall. She laughs, digging through her purse, looking for keys. I overhear her partner and friend talking about making a sauce. "Are you talking about the ghost peppers?" she says. We make a plan to meet, sometime between her busy schedule of kids, shows, and trips to Europe. I can see she's caught somewhere between my questions and the conversation going on about tomatoes at the table beside us. Peter Rowan stands close by, looking older than I remember. His beard is grey, but he's still tall and thin. Julie puts her hand on his back as she returns her beer glass behind the bar. "Yeah, it was a bit of a surprise," Julie says, referring to *Love Tara*'s reissue. "I didn't really know it was coming out."

In June 2015, twenty-three years after it was first released, the stoner rock classic and some say underground masterpiece *Love Tara* was re-released by Sub Pop. Long out of print and fetching top dollar in vinyl-trading circles, this reissue gave old fans a chance to get a copy or replace an old one, and introduced the band to a new generation, those who might not have even been born when the psychedelic rockers were experimenting with their hash-infused sounds in the basements of Moncton, New Brunswick.

Mark was also surprised by *Love Tara*'s re-release. He says he was hoping for an updated version of the album, with some new material. He had talked with Rick years ago about reissuing the album with new songs and previously unreleased music, to make it more interesting for fans. The idea dropped off and they never talked about it again. Mark says they have lots of recorded stuff they could have used. "It's been a while since I've talked to Rick," he says.

III

Rick White has become a bit reclusive and shies away from the spotlight. He still makes music under his own name; he also paints and builds remote-control cars from wood and films them. His Headquake137 YouTube channel is full of videos of cars and trucks and cats in the woods, where he also has a studio. He continues to record bands and friends, Canadian rock royalty like The Sadies and Blue Rodeo, even providing artwork for album covers. Prolific in all things creative, he doesn't see the need to look back on the history of Eric's Trip, its music, and the influence it had on a genre and a generation. Rick's early adoption of lo-fi techniques and DIY gave him time to evolve. Later records with Elevator to Hell were more mature and technical. Never mainstream, that wasn't the goal. But the band and its sound started to take on a feeling, beyond what other bands were doing. They were no longer simply garage rock with low-end tones; they could play their instruments and knew how to adjust the recording devices to make sounds rich and tight.

Rick has become a bit of a legend. His skills are sought after by those looking for something original, fresh, and outside the norm. His Elder Schoolhouse and Blue Fog Recording studio has become a place where bands go to get that "Rick White" sound. Bands like Halifax quartet (now duo) Dog Day, who were heavily influenced by Eric's Trip and Elevator got what they were looking for when they recorded at Rick's studio in March 2009. So much so they named the album *Elder Schoolhouse*. From far and wide, musicians travel there to try and capture what Rick has been doing for years. Over the last few years, he has been recording and producing new solo work, playing all the instruments himself. Along with painting, sketching, and drawing, his life is filled with art on a daily, even hourly, basis.

Although he owns several small businesses and has been involved in record contracts since he was a teenager, Rick is not what you would call a traditional capitalist. More interested in creating, producing, and putting art into the world, he has been known to provide his services for free. He offers his music online for next to nothing. On one Eric's Trip's 7-inch, offered online, he writes: "This is a free download friends, thanks all who have enjoyed my other Bandcamp releases so far. Feel free to give a little if you're doing okay but don't worry about it."

This idea is rooted in the punk rock culture Rick grew up on. Art and commerce have battled it out since the beginning of time, but punk bands never wanted to overcharge for shows, albums, or services (Ian Mackaye of Minor Threat wouldn't play a show in the '80s if the cover at the door was over $5 or $6). The idea of making art for art's sake, punk rock against the establishment, keeping things accessible for everybody has been rooted in punk rock since it began in the '70s.

For Rick, the tradition lives on. It also has something to do with his Moncton roots: we're blue-collar people not wanting to think we're more important than we really are, keeping our egos, work, and ideas in check. For Rick, the idea began in The Underdogs, when the mantra was simply to put music out into the world, and it continues today.

10

THE SCENE
EVOLVES

Moncton has grown a lot since the early 1990s and Eric's Trip's success. The music scene has gotten stronger, venues larger, and more promoters see the city as a viable place to bring touring acts of all sizes. Before the "Seattle of East" moniker given to the area after bands began getting signed out of the Maritimes, few touring acts were willing to take the chance on Moncton or Halifax. But as the area started to get noticed and those in the know gained experience working at and promoting shows, they eventually moved on to more high-profile positions, lending their expertise to major decision makers at The City of Moncton.

Still, the legacy of Eric's Trip continues in the sounds and bands getting up on stage every night in and around Moncton. A music scene has grown and evolved where none existed before. Those who were turned on by Eric's Trip's music and its approach picked up guitars and sat down at drums. The blue-collar concept of plugging away until you find your own sound still exists. It is alive and well in basements, garages, and jam spaces all over Moncton, and beyond. Beer bands and friends jamming, pushing the limits of sound, lyrics, and presentation—some not even born when Rick and his crew started—turned on to the idea there would be an accepting audience, somewhere; a venue to play at, even if it's someone's living room or the back of a record store.

The sense the best bands aren't necessarily the most polished, something Mark Gaudet taught all of us early on, can be found in bands all over the city. The art is in the details and the details aren't overproduced or technical, drowning out the creativity the musicians intended. Instead, everyone is trying to find that natural thing that connects with people. Not the hook or the hype or the tricks used by computers. Not even the repetitive manipulation that plies on your emotional state, assuming you're miserable at work or in a relationship or even in life. No, this music attacks at the core and opens up something carnal inside. It makes you want to jump, scream, and throw your fists into the air, like nobody is watching. It brings us all back to a place where we existed before we got uptight, conservative, and worried about what other people thought. It's the kind of music that isn't safe, has no boundaries, and could erupt at any time. The way music used to be.

III

REMEMBERING ERIC'S TRIP

ANDREW CAMPBELL was a fairly new teacher in 1994 when he got the job to teach media studies at Moncton's new Science and Tech Centre. MacNaughton had been a trades high school with a 95 percent male population for years, focusing on everything from welding to car and body repair. The school board switched gears in the early 1990s, deciding to focus more on computers, content, and the wave of the future.

Starting with a few VCRs, a video camera, and a TV, the school eventually invested $50,000 to create one of the most modern and up-to-date digital media labs in the region. Thinking they could get students to self-promote by making their own videos and music, the district developed a curriculum around the studio. While most were still thinking in analog, Moncton students got a chance to experiment with top-line and progressive recording equipment. Others were also encouraged to come and play, be guinea pigs while everyone was still getting used to the rooms. Only concerned with maintenance, the school charged bands a small fee to rent the soundproof space. "We also accepted trades for use of the studio," Campbell says. "Any music equipment to make the spot better." It became a place to jam, record, write, and hang out.

Nobody knew what would come of this huge investment or if musicians would even use it. Districts often jumped on new ideas, trying to stimulate new directions in education. A lot of times they don't get adapted by staff let alone students. But Campbell knew he had something special here. He had been involved in the music scene and watched it grow since the early '80s. He knew what the kids were into, and had witnessed the trend toward do-it-yourself. Not only did he have a big reception from bands, students wanted to learn the ins and outs of using the equipment. For as many musicians as there were, there were at least as many technicians: guys who liked to set up microphones in the right place, adjust tones for a smoother sound, or take guitars apart and put them back together.

There was a lot of attention and bands began recording their music into the soundboard. Things really ramped up after Rick White came in. "He found ways to record [that] nobody else could," Campbell says. During one session he pointed the mic toward the bass drum, a few feet away. It created an ambiance and a sound everyone tried to copy. After this, everyone wanted Rick to record their demo, album, or song. "It was all about how he used the room," says Campbell.

Most notably, Elevator to Hell used the space for a video shoot. They had a small crane in the auditorium where they shot, using the large space and all the noise and echo it had to offer.

But it wasn't just about sound; the space was also set up with Photoshop and digital printing. Bands had the chance to take photos and manipulate them to create album covers and artwork. CD burning was new at the time and here you could make copies of your music, create a label for the disc, shoot a band photo with a cool background and print it off. It was a full-service space for young musicians who might not have had the chance to do any of these things otherwise. Plus, they were learning a skill, beyond music, that would help a lot of them many years later.

The studio guys, after they got to know the gear, would be paid for their services. There were a few rules and one included paying the technicians a fair wage and paying the school a maintenance fee. Campbell made sure those who were learning the craft didn't do so on a volunteer basis when they were qualified. He was personally logging hundreds of hours of volunteer time but expected the students to earn a little for their expertise. In fact, Campbell often stayed long after school and into the evening and, working through his supper, bands would often bring him a ham and cheese sandwich from Tim Hortons to keep him energized for another night of writing and recording. When it was time to give the studio a name, it didn't take long for someone to suggest Ham & Cheese Studios.

Eventually, students and bands began using other areas of the school to help the recording process. Big open areas with high ceilings made for great sounds, like institutional echos, stuff heard on recent albums like Ministry's *The Mind is a Terrible Thing To Taste* (1989). Andrew and a few others started thinking about how else they could use the building and the next logical step was to put on some shows. In 1995, with the help of those in the know, they organized FuzzFest. A grassroots festival dedicated to the local talent coming through Ham & Cheese studios, FuzzFest was short lived but successful, and because of the hands-on learning environment Andrew had built, everyone got involved. Eric's Trip was nearing the end of their time as a band and didn't play the fest, but all members played with their side projects.

Looking back, Andrew Campbell thinks the Moncton sound also had to do with everybody knowing everyone. This small-town curse turned out to be part of what made bands coming out of Moncton stand out among all others across the country. Having limited venues to play and one or two recording spaces around the city gave them a similar sound, tone, and style—especially when most were asking Rick to be involved.

MacNaughton also hosted Eric's Trip's last show. Ken Kelley was the brains behind it, selling almost all seven hundred tickets available. MuchEast showed up and shone a light not only on Eric's Trip and Sloan but also on some of Moncton's up-and-coming bands. There was a positive vibe in the air, as one era was ending and another was just beginning.

SHANE PORTER is a venue manager with the City of Moncton. He and I went to the first Eric's Trip show together. Skateboarding outside, around the downtown, we heard there was an all-ages show going on and went over. I mostly stood outside, watching the crowd. Shane went in and before we left, we were both fans of Rick's bands and sound. Shane tells me the first time we met we were supposed to fight at a gas station in his neighbourhood. Crowds from different schools had gathered, tough guys pounding their chests, strutting their stuff. All I remember was Shane and I talking about the Descendents. Our love of music anchored our friendship in late elementary; his love of music turned into a career.

"I remember he seemed like a wild guy, but he would talk to everybody," says Shane who, like everyone, has fond memories of visiting Sam The Record Man and Mark Gaudet, learning about what was new in music. From the age of ten, he would go into the store looking for hard rock records. Mark would have an opinion on every purchase and Shane would listen, taking it all in. He remembers how great he felt when Mark would tell his mother, "Your son is on the right track with this music." Mark would talk about the history of rock from England and commend Shane for buying The Dead Kennedys and Black Flag. His mother was also impressed when Mark would strike up a conversation with her about Carole King. He made an impression on everyone he met. These moments set Shane on a path that would lead him to get involved in music and help revolutionize the scene.

After spending a few summers working in events and promotions with the City of Moncton, Shane soon became an asset to the growing needs of Moncton's youth culture. His first real assignment was to help in the organization, design, and construction of the city's first official skateboard park. The ultimate diplomat, he delegated the work to the experts: Moncton's youth. After many meetings chaired by Shane and his team, they built one of the country's best parks. Along Moncton's waterfront, it was the largest and most modern on the east coast when it was built, in 1999. A nice mix of transition, ledges, stairs, and rails, it suits skaters of every age and skill level and it is busy all summer long. And where there is skateboarding, there's music. The rising skateboard scene was connected closely with the music scene still building from what Eric's Trip had created just a few years before.

Local music shows were organized and all-ages shows came together, building the second wave of musicians and bands, those who grew up on '90s music and were now ready to create and put forth their efforts. Shane's background and music obsession proved invaluable.

Within a year the park was full of skateboarders, and older guys who had quit were back. A new skateboard shop, SKATE TO SNOW, had opened; younger kids were playing music again; bands were starting, and the cycle had begun all over again. The one we grew up understanding as young friends in school. Kids were turning up by the hundreds to see bands all over the city. Building on what the bands and the scene of the '80s had created, Shane was now a major part of building and keeping the scene alive. Like the first wave that helped Eric's Trip and Elevator develop their sounds, this new surge was a mix of metal, punk, and folk bands all vying for the attention the country and the world was giving to the Maritimes.

Shane's non-traditional perspective on what could be done for Moncton's youth was catching on. Now responsible for more venues and bigger events, he brought local bands to Canada Day festivities, turning a corner with getting young people back to outdoor City-sponsored activities. He credits the 1997 East Coast Music Awards, held in Moncton, for this rise in interest and attention: "I think it really helped put Moncton on the musical map," he says. Bands like Eric's Trip and Sloan were nationally known by this time and others were getting bigger by the day. Over seven thousand people filled the Moncton Coliseum for the ECMAs and CBC aired the event across Canada, with the who's who of the industry staying downtown, watching live shows featuring all Moncton had to offer. This gave everyone in the city a boost and a chance to ride the wave Eric's Trip had started in 1990.

Now finishing their tenure as the coolest band in the land, Elevator would set the tone for those looking for great music delivered without much fuss. Those who had opened for, and taken their cues from, bands like Eric's Trip and Sloan were now headlining their own shows and playing Moncton's growing list of venues. Throughout the early 2000s, bars and clubs were full nightly with new sounds blended from the past and the future. The do-it-yourself idea had caught on and people everywhere were plugging in. Shane's career was on the move and as he contributed to local music through City events, he also worked with a team who would eventually revamp The Magnetic Hill Concert Site.

As bands like Hope, The Monoxides, Iron Giant, and The Motorleague were building momentum, big-name promoters were starting to take notice of what Moncton had to offer. Lead by Ian Fowler, negotiations began for the biggest concert the city would ever see. In 2005 it was national news that the biggest band in the world, the Rolling Stones, was making a stop in The Hub City. They would play to over eighty thousand fans. After years of struggling for an identity, Moncton was finally creating a name for itself in music, arts, and culture.

French and English cultures were now working together to promote and support events like The Frye Festival, a popular bilingual literary event, and annual food and beer festivals, which attracted thousands to the city each year. After the Rolling Stones, the city followed up with other huge outdoor concerts: AC/DC, The Eagles, Bruce Springsteen, and eventually luring U2 to end their 360 Tour in a field just north of the city. Shane was involved in putting these shows together. From punk rock tapes to seeing Eric's Trip at City Hall, both Shane and the municipality had come a long way.

DANA ROBERTSON grew up in Riverview, New Brunswick, playing baseball and loving music. One of the original members of The Monoxides, he decided to start his own band after seeing Eric's Trip play at an all-ages show in Moncton. Recruiting Chris Lewis on drums and Jamie Oldfield on bass, the band Hope came together in the summer of 1992. Shows were happening everywhere in Moncton—The Shipyard, The Esquire, the Kacho—and the boys wanted to be a part of it. Liking the loud, heavily distorted sound of Eric's Trip and Rick's punk rock roots, they began making noise long before they could play.

Encouraged by the hundreds of kids coming to live shows every week, Hope worked to get on stage. Opening up for friends, they earned their stripes playing show after show and putting together poppy punk rock riffs and catchy lyrics. As the scene got bigger, so did their audiences, and in 1996 they were invited to play Canadian Music Week in Toronto. This helped them get some attention outside the city and led to more gigs. Rick White helped them with a demo, producing and arranging; they were looking for the sound only he could produce: "Rick had his own thing going," Dana says. "It was a different take, very unique." Marco Rocca eventually joined the band, lending some serious riffs, vocals, and songs. Hope went on to sign with a Canadian label, Calgary's Lameass Recordz, touring the Maritimes and eventually across Canada.

Dana thinks Eric's Trip helped unite the punk scene in Moncton and the Maritimes. The country and city came together with those on the fringe. Bands started supporting each other and crowds were mixed with anyone and everyone. This helped bands broaden their appeal, and their audience. The Moncton sound blended together. "Everybody started to know everybody," he says.

It also had something to do with the music everyone grew up on. "I don't know if Mark Gaudet gets enough credit," adds Dana, who grew up at the mall, listening and getting to know Mark. He was always impressed with how supportive Mark was of the local scene. He would see Mark at every gig, buying everyone's demos. Usually on everybody's guest list, he still paid, understanding the importance of supporting gigs. Dana remembers buying Judas Priest and Ozzy Osbourne tapes at Sam's and Mark giving him the nickname "Peanut." He also remembers Mark as an encyclopedia of music.

Because everyone was listening to the music Mark recommended every week and meeting through music and skateboarding, the sounds were blending together and the kids picking up instruments were all on the same page. Mark not only set the tone with his own bands, he laid a foundation for the youth of the city to have an ear for what was good, important, and relevant in music. Over thirty-five years of pushing kids in the right direction has had a huge impact on what people recognize as the Moncton sound and scene.

Hope went on to tour, including playing the Vans Warped Tour, and Dana still remembers how it all got started. Hearing Eric's Trip and their simple choices to leave squeaky drum pedal sounds or a chair falling over in their music, encouraged him and his friends to do what they were doing. Three-chord songs and home recordings was the goal. Big light shows and production wasn't on anyone's radar. Creating the perfect album became more about creating something on their own.

CHRIS LEWIS grew up in Lakeside Estates, on the outskirts of the city: a rough neighbourhood with tough kids, where fighting and heavy metal were a rite of passage. His early bands, Frost Bite, Skinkeeper, and Iron Giant, would blend metal with punk and help create the sound Moncton would become known for. Chris was determined to make his way into the scene from an early age and wanted to get his music noticed one way or another. He became a student of the local scene, watching how bands set up, played, and presented their shows. He loved it all and understood there was something real to the raw, no-bullshit, stripped-back Moncton sound. "I made up for any lack of talent with enthusiasm," Chris says in his backyard, planning an upcoming European tour with his new band, Zaum.

Chris noticed local bands didn't do a lot of guitar solos and the drumming was hard-hitting and pure, with no fillers. He brought this straight ahead approach back to his own band practices. Not liking to spend a ton of time rehearsing, he deliberately kept his sound barbaric, not wanting to overplay. For Chris, it was more about the feeling you put into it and going with your gut. He wasn't interested in how technical and flamboyant you could be. This idea was planted in the heads of Moncton musicians way back and has never left. "It all started with Mark [Gaudet]," Chris says.

Chris Lewis has been making music with friends since the mid-'80s and hasn't stopped. Rick White produced and recorded some of Chris's early bands, like Mood Cadillac in 1997. Rick also helped Chris design album covers and gig posters and was responsible for "that sound," evolved from Mark Gaudet's early '80s punk bands. "We often recorded stuff in one take, mistakes and all." Chris says. "The mistakes were part of the beauty of it."

Now, Chris plays with and helps to develop the next generation of bands. He also provides a crucial service rarely talked about among touring acts. One that is essential to a band's survival, especially in Canada.

On an un-assuming street on the fringes of Moncton's downtown sits a house surrounded by trees, fences and a porch. Bikes are everywhere, stickers on the door. This is a band house, like those found in any city across the country. A place where locals and touring musicians can stop, make a pot of KD, and party with friends. Chris lives here and he owns one of the most unique band houses on the planet.

A bouncer in some of Moncton's toughest bars for most of his adult life, Chris Lewis has created a musical shrine with three dogs. The walls are decorated with band, tour, and venue posters of the now half a dozen configurations he's played with. Framed pictures of icons line the halls like a heavy metal Musée d'Art.

Turtles, snakes, and other creatures share the space, adding to the ambiance. The fridge is covered with stickers, something you'd expect to find in a house where there is a full bar. Not a '70s stand-behind like your parents had, a full, working six-seater, complete with taps and a Jägermeister machine.

Upstairs, a bass hangs off the wall: a tribute to a childhood friend who killed himself, the Hall-of-Fame-like atmosphere a perfect memorial for Sandy LeClair, who would love to be remembered among all this music history.

A short walk brings you to the master bedroom, decorated in a bullfighter's motif. A velvet painting over the headboard, a red throw covering the bed. The room is full of knickknacks, bullhorns, and sombreros. Vans shoeboxes are stacked on the floor.

His office is across the hall, the perfect place to scribble words for his new Middle Eastern Doom band, Zaum. He's a drummer, singer, and showman who's proud of his "east coast white trash" roots, a slogan he uses to connect with others who've chosen a life in music.

The bathroom is something else—some might say, where the magic really happens. It's a modest space, with all the things you'd expect. Toilet, shower, tub, sink. Storage for all your needs. But this room is different, almost holy. What started out as a few trinkets has turned into an obsession. Wall to wall Jesus pictures, figurines, and everything else Christ. It's like a church on acid. A Bible sits on the back of the toilet, propping up a praying-hands cast. A copy of *Highway to Hell* blends in nicely with a few versions of the good book.

Musicians from near and far come to do their business in this bathroom. It's a meditative space, some might even say religious. Ideas flow here like the inner workings of good digestion. It's spots like this that are fuelling the independent movement of rock and roll in this country.

Music is prime for another revolution. It doesn't take executives to figure out why people aren't buying records anymore. The music being made by bands like Zaum, Which Witch is Which, and thousands of others like them, in small clubs and bars, are what people are interested in. If you want to find the real pulse of music in this country, find your local band house, dive music venue, or underpaid, overly enthusiastic musician working at a record store. These places and people will tell you about the next great band. Chances are you haven't heard about them. Chances are they will be your next favourite.

TARA LANDRY-WHITE grew up in Alberta. Her parents were displaced east coasters who started a Maritime Club with their friends, playing music, having lobster races, and putting on live shows. She remembers hearing lots of traditional folk and Celtic music growing up, as well as Buffy Sainte-Marie, The Beatles, and Simon & Garfunkel. Just before she started high school, her family moved to Moncton. They lived in a big, old character house her great-grandparents had built on a hill near the university. Bridging her early days at Moncton High by joining a band, she made friends quickly. Her brother played in his own band so there were instruments around. One day, she picked up a bass and started practicing in her room, with Fugazi and The Breeders as some of her first inspirations. She was in her late teens in 1995 when she joined a band with a few friends and they called themselves Collide. In 1996 they morphed into Orange Glass with Ron Bates on guitar and Chris Flanagan on drums.

Moncton's music scene was small but growing in 1993, and bands were always interested in what other musicians were doing. Tara decided to write a letter to Rick White, someone she only knew from seeing around school but was attracted to because of his look, creativity, and growing reputation as an artist. Once she made contact with him and Julie, they all became friends, groups morphing and scenes converging.

Tara and Rick became closer as time went on and the tension and conflict created a rift between young friends. Guilt complicated Rick's love for Julie, and his ability to use her as a muse. He put it all down on paper and turned it into the Sub Pop release *Love Tara*, outlining a conflicted young artist with a new inspiration. This new attention didn't sit well with Landry. Having the record named after her, being put on the cover, and thrown into the middle of the drama was a lot to handle. "I was a bit overwhelmed," says Tara during a phone interview from her home on the west coast. "It was a tumultuous time."

But the transition continued. With Rick's attention focused on Tara and Eric's Trip rising in popularity, Rick began working on a solo album. These solo recordings would eventually become the first Elevator to Hell record and lead to Rick playing more with Tara and Mark. The more popular Eric's Trip got, the more Rick retreated to the heavier, psychedelic underground of Elevator. Tara says Rick began feeling increased pressure to tour and play, and this only sent him deeper inward.

For Rick, the jams with Tara and Mark became a bit of a retreat. There was no pressure to sound like anything in particular; it was experimenting with friends in the basement all over again. With no agenda and no interest in commercializing their music, Elevator kept playing and writing songs. They were all enjoying the less popular, heavier sound and the freedom to take it in any direction.

Rick sent the Elevator demo to Sub Pop on a whim; when they released it, the band started to take things more seriously. As Eric's Trip was wrapping up with everyone going their separate ways, Rick was putting more songs and time into Elevator. It was now clear how things were going to end, and Tara started feeling even guiltier. "I wish things would have worked out different," she says. "It all became a bit too much."

Elevator eventually geared up to tour in promotion of their new project. Always heading from point A to point B, there was never anytime to sightsee, explore, or get to know any of the places you were visiting. Hours and hours of driving to get to a town to play a show, then often back on the road. "It felt like we worked all day long," Tara remembers. It was worth it when the band stepped up on stage and people showed up to hear them play. It was great to be out there, playing together. "I still miss it," says Tara. "I loved playing with those guys."

Tara can't say enough about Mark and Rick as musicians and friends. She calls Mark "one of the best drummers in North America." She considers him more of a sibling than a friend. Like every other young music fan in Moncton, she remembers hanging around in the mall and visiting Mark at Sam's. Getting schooled on everything local and beyond. He also tried to make her blush with crazy stories only he could tell. This would serve her well being stuck in a van with him criss-crossing Canada in the '90s. She puts it simply: "Mark doesn't try to be, he just is."

On the road, Tara acted as manager for the band, dealing with money and finances. Keeping track of money, mapping out routes, booking shows, and long drives were exhausting. Living off of less than $20 a day and little sleep made tour life tough. Rick and Mark didn't want a middleman and didn't trust anyone outside the band to have their best interests at heart. This was one area that stressed Tara out:

making money last and getting from one place to the next, always on the cheap, kept her in a state of constant worry. This made it hard to enjoy the whole experience.

Rick, meanwhile, was concerned with creating something every day, and not so much with money. Still isn't. Tara admits this made things tough on their marriage at times. She tried to get him to work "real" jobs but his concern was always for his music and art. Even when they were broke and living in Toronto, and with Elevator not doing much, Rick continued to struggle against the confines of organized society. Tara says it comes from his punk rock roots: "He's one of the most adversarial [people] you will ever meet."

With Elevator's popularity rising following the Sub Pop release, Rick did not like the attention; he felt like he was selling out, playing to growing crowds and more diverse fans. The songs were very personal and meant a lot to him. He felt odd sharing them with others, feeling obligated to tour and promote the music. Ironically, Tara believes this is why people liked the music so much and why it's still valued all these years later: there was mystery to it. Rick was elusive and let the art do the talking. They also didn't press and release many copies of the records, so it made them hard to find and in turn more attractive.

Tara also sees how much influence Rick had on others. Kids were tired of the commercialism of music in the early '90s and Eric's Trip and Elevator showed it could be done with more effort and passion than money. His DIY ethos and need to create had a huge influence on the Moncton scene and many scenes around the world. "It pioneered a lot of people to do a similar thing," she says.

Tara now lives a quiet life on Vancouver Island with her partner and family nearby. Her brother plays in a few bands—more folk now than punk or metal. She still talks about playing, creating, and finding more time to develop that side of her life. For now, she looks back on her time in Elevator with pride. Fairly limited releases of their albums make them a collector's dream, with some fetching over $150 online. A Facebook search of the band and Eric's Trip shows thousands of fans from all over the world.

Elevator's music and reputation is still alive and well in the internet age; part of the mystery surrounding them was due to the lack of information available to fans in the 1990s, as the internet was just coming into its own. This mysterious allure was only accentuated by how few interviews the band did, their sporadic touring, and a lack of interest in self-promotion. Both Eric's Trip and Elevator were pretty introverted and shy, preferring to let the music do most of the talking. They were also the last of a dying breed of artists who were interested in keeping parts of their music sacred; not everything was meant to be shared. In the new-media world, where we get to see people's movements twenty-four hours a day, there is not much left to the imagination. We know so much about every song, band, and artist; we know the meaning behind everything, there's no mystery anymore. There's also no originality left when everybody starts to love a band for the same reasons or everything sounds the same. Real art makes you stop.

STEVEN MCDONALD remembers playing in Moncton with Eric's Trip. His band Redd Kross would have a huge influence on the crossover from punk in the '80s to alternative music in the early '90s and beyond. Coming out of California music culture, he and his brother Jeff would shake up the scene on the west coast with their third album and major-label debut, *Third Eye*. Bands like Redd Kross began breaking down the wall from punk rock to alternative and gave everybody license to make the music they wanted to make, especially within the underground scene. Before this, it was easy to get sucked in to the trap of only wanting to reach a certain audience: those in the know. This was great for those who were dedicated to one sound or one genre, but for musicians and artists like Redd Kross and Eric's Trip, it took the fun out of making music.

The two bands toured together across the UK in the fall of 1993. Though new to European audiences, both played to enthusiastic crowds. Audiences were open minded and eager to new musical approaches.

McDonald recalls Eric's Trip's sound and stage show: "I remember they didn't use house lights, they had lamps without shades," he says. He found they had a real Sonic Youth influence that was uniquely Canadian: he liked the back and forth between Rick and Julie's voices and thought the band was friendly and fun, describing their sound as mellow with "cool melodic guitar." McDonald also remembers Rick telling him they got a grant from the Canadian government to help pay for expenses to tour the UK; he couldn't believe the country offered their artists money to tour and promote their music. "It was surreal to me," he says.

Redd Kross joined Eric's Trip for some Maritime shows that same year, and the narrow roads and highways through New Brunswick have left a lasting impression on McDonald. He remembers it was very thickly wooded. At one point, the band noticed something running on the side of the road, next to their van. It jumped out and clipped the side of the vehicle. Everyone paid more attention after that. Far away from home at the time, the feeling of being somewhere unique in North America wasn't lost on Redd Kross while spending time in Moncton and Halifax. "Most California bands don't get out of California," says McDonald.

He remembers most of Eric's Trip being fairly quiet and shy: "They were meek, mild, sweet, and fun." Except the drummer, who was outgoing and boisterous. They talked about bands and music and cracked jokes about the lifestyle they lived. Mark had been a fan of Redd Kross for years and enjoyed every second he spent with the McDonald brothers. "Mark and I were obsessed with SunChips," Steven says. "We laughed a lot, I remember that."

Wearing an Eric's Trip T-shirt on stage after playing with them got McDonald a few nods from people in strange places across Canada. He's not surprised that the band has since become an underground legend. He remembers the rumour they were going to play together again at Pop Montreal around 2011: "I was excited about it and disappointed it didn't happen," he says. Clearly, he is not alone.

IAN MACKAYE knows a few things about opening up the world to his scene, his music, and voice. He and his friends, who included Henry Garfield—better known as Henry Rollins—were tired of feeling isolated in their hometown of Washington, D.C. They were tired of hearing about bands from L.A., New York, and Chicago, so they created their own scene. They brought their isolation to the rest of the country through music, lyrics, and a record label known the world over. Today, Ian Mackaye is known as one of the originators of the American hardcore punk scene, and a founding member of the heavily influential bands Minor Threat and Fugazi. Together these bands paved the way for most underground rock to thrive in a world fascinated with radio hits and mainstream success.

In 1980 Mackaye started the short-lived but hugely groundbreaking band Minor Threat. Based on the DIY aesthetic initiated by Black Flag, the band became known for its straight-edge values, countering the teen-angst, partying, and drinking philosophy of the time. Opting for more righteous ideas, like becoming knowledgeable about things important to you and spreading good positive vibes, the band helped raise the consciousness of a new generation of young people within the punk rock community.

The band was also one of the first to self-promote, do their own bookings, and create their own road map of venues all across North America without the use of promoters, managers, or agents. Building on the foundations laid by Greg Ginn of Black Flag and Canadian bands like Vancouver's DOA, who came a few years before them, they would set the tone for all bands who came after.

I talked to Mackaye about Canadian music and the shift from the '80s to the '90s. He's a big fan of Canadian music and thinks some of the best bands come from obscure areas. He puts it simply: "Ideas come from small towns; sales come from big cities." This is part of his theory: that some of the best bands come from smaller, out of the way places, where good ideas have time to cultivate and grow. He tells me about the DC scene before the '80s, and how Washington was basically known as a government town, federal and culturally small.

His company, Dischord Records, did a lot to change that. Recently celebrating its thirty-fifth anniversary, Dischord's aim has always been to build the local scene, one band at a time.

Originally intended to promote Mackaye's early bands, Dischord spread to support local Washington bands and created a scene where one didn't exist. Before the label, people were listening to Top 40 and cooperate rock on the radio. The same as everywhere else in the country. "When I got into punk rock," says Mackaye, "I turned my radio off forever."

Dischord and Minor Threat were as much of a statement as they were anything else. A middle finger to the mainstream and choice to make it despite everyone and everything. Known for challenging their audiences with smart, thoughtful lyrics, they also made it a point to keep ticket prices low. Mackaye tried for years to keep admission to his shows, both for Fugazi and Minor Threat, around $5. He wanted anyone and everyone to attend, believing a show should be a give and take between the band and the audience.

On a trip through the Maritimes in the summer of 1998, Fugazi played a few shows in Fredericton and Halifax. The crowds were enthusiastic and eager and Ian remembers picking up a couple of hitchhikers on the way to the venue. They were young guys, punked out in the traditional leather jacket and patches. They got in the car and started talking about the Fugazi show, wondering if the band was even going to show up. They were pumped that a hardcore band from away had come to their small town and couldn't believe they were going to see Ian Mackaye. Unaware he was sitting in the front seat and firing questions at them, and surrounded by gear and the stench of a band who had been on tour all summer, they began to get quieter as they approached the rec centre where the show was happening. "I think the penny had dropped for one of them," says Mackaye. "He realized who we were."

Even now, Mackaye still talks about the time like he didn't create this world for all of us to enjoy and build upon. He tells stories about Fugazi and Black Flag with as much excitement as I do and I get the sense he would talk music all day. He mentions bands and musicians like Eric's Trip, those who play because they love music. The ones who would be playing if they couldn't tour, make any money, or get record contracts. These are the bands he most admires. These are the musicians he thinks are most important: "It's music that has to happen," he says.

He talks about a fairly recent trip to Cape Breton, for a friend's fortieth birthday. They visited the island and got a sense of the traditional music from the area. He made the connection between the scene and bands like Eric's Trip who worked to create it when nobody took it seriously. From an area of the world nobody really knew. "They were doing it because they wanted to do it," he says.

Mackaye remembers Eric's Trip and the wave of original bands and music that swept through the early 90s. Fugazi was focused on their work and avoided the mass media onslaught and attempt to categorize bands and genres. It was less about music at the time and more about big business trying to capture the next big thing. Bands were shifting their sound, focused on how they presented themselves, moving to Seattle, worried how much their contracts were worth. The environment was changing rapidly. Bands now focused on hits and fiscal success began to lose focus. They started to get screwed over with bad contracts, as the frenzy to find the next Nirvana tied too many bands in to forever and a day.

Being in a place of obscurity and under the radar worked for Dischord and bands like Eric's Trip. They weren't close enough to the big suck to get pulled in and also weren't tempted by false hopes and dreams. Even some of the most virtuous bands in punk rock got lured into major label dreams and some argue it changed them as a band. When you accept a large advance, the bigger it is and the longer the contract, the more expectations there are for you to pay it back. You're basically in debt to the record company before you ever see a profit. And every cent they give you to tour, record, or advertise your music keeps you a slave to them for good.

Mackaye believes sitting down to write and record music must have an effect on bands when they know they're under the gun right from the beginning. This has to change their approach and ideas of the kind of music they write. It would be hard to be focused on art and making the music you want to make when you have people hanging over you expecting you to produce. This pressure could even be felt in the type of distribution a major label would want for your band. Will your songs, albums, and lyrics get into the family friendly stores where they will be seen? Or will they sit shy and alone on the shelves of a quiet record store somewhere, waiting to be found? Is it better to reach a small amount of devoted, true fans, who really appreciate the art in your record, even though the amount to make it, record it, and tour it is probably more than you'll make on sales? Or do you take the risk a big company might get behind you and push you to the front of a megastore and put you out on a big tour and sales might someday cover all your expenses? Better yet, you get a radio or viral hit and you make a little money, enough to keep working on music and record another album. Then it starts again, another catchy song, as good or better than "Who Let the Dogs Out."

This idea is not practical, Mackaye says. Having big overhead, and charging a lot at the door to cover it, forces you to play the songs the audiences wants to hear: "I don't want to have to entertain," he says, "I want to play what I want."

Mackaye and his wife have been playing shows with their band, The Evens, since 2001. They're an evolution from his days in hardcore and punk rock. More indie sounding, they continue the same traditions Mackaye has been advocating since his early days: "I want to make it a conversation," he says.

The man himself has mellowed as time has passed. He's not looking to tear down the system the way he once did, he simply wants to continue promoting good music without any outside influence. He sees a world much better off without mass culture, mass media, and mass consumption. Happy to provide people who understand where art comes from with music made by people who take the time to really work at it, he still plugs away at the Dischord House the same way he's done since 1980.

KEITH MORRIS is a California punk rock legend. He not only co-founded Black Flag with Greg Ginn, some say was the heart and soul of the band. Considered to be one of the first punk rock bands, period, and one of America's first hardcore bands, Black Flag formed in 1976 in Hermosa Beach, California. Though their life as a band was short—less than ten years—what they created in the decade between 1976 and '86 was a culture and a legacy for bands like Eric's Trip to build on.

Creative differences with Ginn saw Morris leave Black Flag in 1979, and he went on to form two other hugely influential bands, Circle Jerks (1979) and Off! (2009). Born in Hermosa Beach, California, Morris was at the centre of the Los Angeles punk scene when it began to blossom in the late '70s. He began his punk life by hanging around "The Strand," a paved bicycle path/boardwalk that runs along the Pacific Coast and LA beach communities. He developed a real liking for drugs and music at an early age and is known for his long dreadlocks, slow, west coast drawl, and hard-partying lifestyle.

At age sixty, Morris is still working hard to encourage kids to get out there and live it: "Turn your computer off," he says, "go be a part of the experience." He thinks we sit around and complain too much about things that aren't important—like which bands plays with each other or what music you're allowed to listen to if you like punk rock. "In the '80s, we were confined," he says. "The punk rock police and ethics committee said we couldn't play with certain bands." Music, according to Morris, should be about what feels good.

Morris remembers his brother and sister having big record collections: everything from Styx to Journey to Kansas; he got rid of a lot of those records when everyone was so concerned about being a punk rock purist. When Off! formed in 2009, the punk rock supergroup made up of Dimitri Coats (Burning Brides), Steven McDonald (Redd Kross), and Mario Rubalcaba (Rocket from the Crypt), the band decided they were going to intentionally play with bands nobody expected them to play with. They didn't want to limit themselves or be forced into any kind of category. They were all just happy to be playing again and that people still came out to hear it.

"You get stuck when everyone starts to look alike and sound alike," says Morris.

Though they later got flack for mixing with today's modern music, Off! played the 2015 Coachella Valley Music and Arts Festival. Morris admits he wasn't sure about the gig at first. But after seeing what happened to the Vans Warped Tour and coming to grips with Punk Rock Bowling, The Punk Rock Museum, and everything else working to cultivate a nostalgia for the music of his past, he was OK with it. He wasn't happy getting criticized by the punk rock purists. "It brings a bunch of like-minded people together," he says of the fest. "And the Coachella guys started booking punk rock shows way back in the day."

Today there are so many new bands and sounds and Morris is excited to see what's out there. He's always been a fan of exposing people to new bands and thinks these mixed festivals are continuing to do that. "[People] may come to see Off! and leave with a new favourite band," he says. He's over the old, bitter, single-minded fans, and thinks they could all benefit from stretching their tastes a bit; he thinks everyone is missing out on up-and-coming music. Morris is also happy to tip his hat to older bands, those who laid the foundation in rock, and thinks they all should have access to play to bigger crowds. Big music festivals continue to give new bands that chance. "I like being someone's connection to the past," he says. "And introducing them to new bands like TV on the Radio."

Never shy to express his opinion or challenge conventional views, Morris encourages everyone to pick up a guitar, bass or drumsticks, start a band, sing; create your own scene, ideas, destiny, and legacy. At the very least, get out to shows, be involved, make stuff happen. He and his bands always felt on the edge of music, on the fringe looking in. Always wanting to be a part of it. Now, they're happy they can be.

Morris worries people sit and observe too much. Watching everything online and never really listening to music in a personal way. Everything moves so quickly now, and people don't often give albums or bands a real chance. The hit machine has turned us all into observers, not true appreciators of music as art. Morris wants people to remember what it's like to be in a sweaty, crowded, stinky club. Standing with a drink in your hand, with your friends, excited to see what's going to happen. He thinks the tension and excitement is lost when you aren't experiencing a live show. That feeling, when the lights go off and the band comes on stage: "There's a heaviness in the air," he says, of that moment, "it's like a celebration."

There is an anger in the room, from the band and the crowd; it changes how the musicians perform. You can't see it or feel it but you know it's there. All kinds of like-minded people, standing, shouting, waiting for something. This is what gets into your head and makes you want to pick up a guitar yourself. These moments are what change a person, a band, a city, and a scene. It's these moments that propel people to get out and do something. Morris puts it simply: "You need to hang out in a parking lot, smoke some cigarettes, and drink some beer."

There are too many people simply watching it all happen. Complaining about what it should or shouldn't be. Those who aren't contributing anything or helping change it. In the late '70s, unhappy with the direction of current music on the radio, guys like Keith Morris, Ian MacKaye, Lee Ranaldo, and Steve MacDonald went out and created the sounds they wanted to hear. None of them knew the impact they would have on generations of kids and the pushback punk rock would help create. It struck a chord with all those kids who weren't into sports, disco, school, or fitting in. These were the kids feeling alienated from everyone around them, those who couldn't fake it so others would like them. "We just wanted kids to carpool in from the suburbs and experience what it was like," Morris says. "We wanted them to make something happen."

In the case of Moncton, that very thing became the catalyst for the scene that continues to grow. Those who live all around the city come in with their instruments and meet others who play. They all get together now, tired of the music on the radio or in the charts, and grind out a new sound. Hopefully, those in the crowd are thinking of what comes next and are plotting the same idea, so the next generation can make its way to the front. The way Eric's Trip did in 1990.

III

It's starting to happen again: Glimmers of what was and what could be again. Those shining moments rarely seen. Off the backs of what Eric's Trip started almost thirty years ago. I saw it last Saturday night at Moncton's Esquire Tavern.

Nearly a hundred people gathered, drinking Schooner and Alpine: an east coast tradition. Most of us cynical about the state of rock music. My recent attempt at irony and anti-hipsterism on Facebook boasted, *Rock and Roll, I'm not mad, just disappointed*. As I stood in my Ramones T-shirt, high-top Vans, and trucker hat at forty-two.

Then it happened.

Three young guys, Richie Bourbon, Dave Belliveau, and Billy Leblanc, self conscious in their ability, looking at the stage, shaking in the light, making snide remarks to the crowd, trying to hide their nervous energy. The singer—tight jeans, Vans, and long hair—from a different era rips into the crowd. He lays it out there, heart on his sleeve, demons and all. I've known this kid for years and I've admired his don't-care attitude. But he's vulnerable; a paradox, like any great artist.

"We're the fucking Disasterbaters," he screams into the mic as the stage lights illuminate his face.

This is energy. This is living. Millions of dollars in production, a billion people watching worldwide—those shows can't capture this for one minute. The crowd moves back and forth, a culture of arm and arm patched jackets and coloured hair. Most pushed to the fringe by those who don't understand them, preferring this space on the edge, looking in. These kids, the true underdogs in society, have an instinct for life; they're in perfect position to surprise everyone around them.

Behind a cardboard sign that reads THREE-DOLLAR JÄGERMEISTER, the bartender scrambles to fill orders. Lines grow in every direction. The bass player pushes hair out of his face, slapping his Gibson to carry sound. The drummer hits hard with a smile on his face. The sound is raw energy. A few beers, a little off, from the gut, something you can't practice or fake. This is what the music industry is missing. A young woman with green hair and a leather jacket sings every word. She stands at the front of the stage, happier than I've ever seen anyone. Her friends stand beside her, arms in the air, committed, stoked, and passionate. The way I used to feel about music.

After the show, the room is still moving. Energy pushing through the feet, hands, and hips of those who can't let go of what they just heard. Ritchie comes over and apologizes for his voice and the band not sounding so good. I tell him it was amazing. He might not realize it yet, but it might never sound better. Bigger venues, more production, money, managers, fame, and more fans will only ruin what he and his friends have on this cold Saturday night in February. Whatever they were looking for when they first got together, I can tell you, they've already found.

11

RESISTING THEIR LEGACY

On a visit to Sydney, Australia, in 2006, ten years after Eric's Trip have broken up, I step down into a basement music store. The place smells like old records, dust, and male obsessive compulsion. Flipping through vinyl and enjoying the uninviting music on the overhead speakers, I notice a large poster hanging on the wall. The long hair, plaid shirts, and jean jackets catch my eye and I do a double take when I realize it's the kids from my neighbourhood. Eric's Trip had made its way to the other side of the world. I walk over to the quiet, eyes-half-closed clerk behind the counter and ask him about the poster.

"I love Eric's Trip," he says.

We spend an hour talking music, stoner rock, and the origin of Moncton and the New Brunswick music scene. He tells me their albums are imports in Australia, hard to get, sought after, expensive, and quick to sell. Prized possessions for those in the know. He talks about the band as if they are a myth, their music unattainable for some; those who had it kept it close, not even willing to share it, wanting to keep the secret just between friends. I tell him about early releases, demos and cassettes you could only get in and around Moncton, and he looks interested and a bit jealous. The collector in him knows how precious something like this would be among friends—not financially, just for bragging rights.

III

Eric's Trip's legacy can still be felt more than twenty-five years after they started as a band in the basement of Chris Thompson's house in the west end of Moncton. Bands young and old take the spirit of what Rick, Julie, Ed, Mark, and Chris started and they try to recreate it every night, somewhere, either on stage, in their bedroom, or in a jam space. Friends getting together, adjusting microphones on four tracks, with pawn shop instruments, doing it themselves in one take, breaking down the barriers that hold people back.

Looking around Moncton, it's even clearer how much impact Eric's Trip has had and continues to have. Kids walking with guitar cases, skateboarders with painted grip tape, Mark still preaching at Frank's Music, selling the gospel of music to all those who will listen. The scene has grown and changed but what drives people has remained the same. Few musicians or bands in the city are looking for fame or fortune. Most are looking to play with friends, write some songs to express themselves for fun and creativity. You don't see that simplicity and close-knit drive to keep a scene intact everywhere. There is competition, but it's friendly. Everyone wants to see everyone else get better. It's not about outdoing the next guy.

Bands welcome those coming up and support each other. The elders, guys like Chris Lewis, Don Levandier, and Ray 13, make sure the young bands get their due and play shows, and that people know about them. Because not that long ago, they were the young guys. There's always a lull in the scene, like in any city or town. This often has to do with venues and all-ages availability. Moncton has done a great job keeping this up with guys like Shane Porter, who works for the city and has a love and interest in keeping bands playing. There's also been a huge effort by local record stores like Spin-It and its owner, Pat Parise, who host in-store shows. Then there's the ultimate punk rock haven: Claude's House, a jam space turned rock venue. Simply a house where locals gather to play, drink, and have fun, with the motto *You're only punk once*. Well said.

III

For a band who started trying to do things differently than everyone else, it all came full circle in 2009, when Eric's Trip was inducted into Canada's Independent Music Hall of Fame. The goal of the organization is to highlight the country's independent musicians, those who might not want or be able to get attention from other award-granting organizations. Two artists are chosen annually and with, a jury made up of music journalists across the country, a band is chosen. The criteria for entry is simple: the band or artist must be Canadian, boldly encourage the spirit of independent music, and have released at least one album on an indie label.

Eric's Trip certainly met the criteria and in some ways brought it to the forefront. Almost afraid of bringing their music too close to the mainstream, they battled between staying under the radar and breaking up. Never expecting to become anything more than a small band who played parties and the odd bar show, Eric's Trip began to revolt against the attention their indie cred brought them. Wanting to remain small, obscure, and mysterious is a battle when you create something and put it out into the world. The moment you share your philosophy with others, you're bound to find people who agree. What nobody knew was how much people would relate to and want to become a part of the world Eric's Trip was creating.

They were awarded with another honour in 2014, this time a Lifetime Achievement Award from Music New Brunswick for their work to help support and promote music within the province. Music NB called the band "our most successful export," and recognized them for "their quiet, unassuming and seemingly insular work ethic." Almost twenty years after the band broke up, those a step away from what actually happened started to recognize the kind of influence Eric's Trip had on New Brunswick. It also took this long for the province to recognize the importance of promoting and supporting its own.

There was a time when people only cared about music playing on the radio and in the Top 40. Now we see smaller bands with strong roots to culture. Making sure there is room for up and coming bands and musicians is not only good sense, but it can be good for our regional economy, and for exposing the outside world to our culture.

III

For artists like Rick, Julie, Chris, and Mark, the consequence of making the music you want on your own terms, without compromise, is a life of struggle. Dedicating your life to the arts that we all take for granted, expecting music to be at our fingertips. Art is made by people who have given up the chance at regular paycheques, stability, daytime working hours—all the things people think are necessary for the world to function.

We need people who see the world differently. We need people like Rick White, who work non-stop to make us realize that whoever is performing at the Grammys are not the only musicians in the world, and thank dog. We need people like Julie Doiron to continue the tradition of the oral storyteller, keeping bars and theatres full, singing to us about love and the human condition. We need people like Chris Thompson, who keep pushing music in different directions, with new bands, so we don't forget that independent music isn't a bad word, that it's a living breathing thing that needs to be pushed, pulled, moulded, and sculpted often, so it doesn't stagnate and become Aerosmith. And we need people like Mark Gaudet, the person we all want to be, who lives and breathes music, works in a record store, and continues to raise the youth of our cities, ensuring they don't get lost in the Top 40 radio garbage being thrown at them daily.

We need bands like Eric's Trip and Elevator to Hell to help us remember not everything is for sale. There's a reason we look to bands like them. There's no bullshit, no corruption, and they fight against everything we don't want to happen. They help us believe art still exists, somewhere. And there's a chance we could go out and make it too. Eric's Trip and Elevator make us feel like there's hope for music in a world where the entitled get rich and the talented stay faceless and unknown. And maybe that's for the best.

OUTRO

'm forty-two now and still wearing Vans, jeans, and a punk rock T-shirt. I went skateboarding this morning, and although I can't move the same way I used to and my hair is not as radical—in fact it's pretty much short and boring—I still see the world the same way. I still listen to the same music, I still see lines along the streets and sidewalk I would like to skate on. The rooms in my house are filled with guitars, basses, extra skateboards, and records. I have about a dozen pairs of Vans on rotation all the time and spend my time in dingy bars watching bands that play for love, not money. And, I still don't care for authority. Not much has changed.

We turn the lights on, heading downstairs to the basement. A *Thrasher Magazine* flag covers the window and a big grey carpet on the cement floor protects drums, amps, and guitar cases from scratches and dirt. Life has come full circle for us, playing in a punk band, middle aged in a house I own. Shane Porter, PJ Dunphy, and I settle in with a few beers and some chips, a Saturday night ritual when we can. We get together at Ian's too, a similar jam space set up in his basement a couple of hours' drive away. Kids' toys, strollers, and life make it more difficult, but Ferg and I make the trip, sit and listen to old punk records, go skateboarding, and talk old times.

Distortion pedals plugged in, we find a groove that is deep, dark, and dirty. Not as fast as those we loved as kids: slower now, more melodic but with the same angry undertones. Shane doesn't look any different than he did thirty years ago. He's wearing a snowboard T-shirt, Vans, and a trucker hat. The smile on his face tells me he's not worried about his mortgage, truck payment, or Monday meetings. His foot tapping on the floor and a tallboy of hipster beer are signs we're off to a good start.

The moment PJ picks up his guitar it's clear what he was meant to do. Three decades of bass riffs and countless albums and tours tell their own story. The pressures of crowds, who's who, and how many albums sold are non-existent tonight. The only one to judge is Charlie, my eight-year-old pug. Melissa joins us on rhythm guitar. She's got every Misfits and Ramones tune on lock.

Skateboards still lean against the wall, none of us much different than we were when we discovered punk rock. A little wider through the waistline, some of us with a little less hair, but our spirit is the same. Sitting behind the drum kit I hear the jam come together when everyone gets on the same page—"when the magic happens," as Mark Gaudet would say. We're all smiling, nodding our heads, hands moving fast up the fretboards. I'm flailing from snare to hi-hat to crash.

We never expected music would have such a huge impact on our lives, guide our decisions the way it has. In one way or the other we've all shaped our lives around it. We tell old stories and laugh about our youth. All the while I'm sweating to keep up. My feet move fast, offbeat, while my hands thrash around like a mad man's. It sounds like it sounds and nobody cares because there's nowhere we'd rather be. We're doing what every band, everywhere in the world starting out does: we're having fun.

ACKNOWLEDGEMENTS

Music changed my life. This story is one of thousands I could have told but it's a significant one. The people I met through skateboarding, listening to punk rock and Eric's Trip are some of my closest friends. Not only that, they still inspire me every day. Moncton often gets lost to larger centres in Canada and the US, to bigger, cooler scenes, and ignored in the big picture. Rick White, Chris Thompson, Ed Vaughan, Julie Doiron and Mark Gaudet helped change all that and we have them to thank. Watching and listening to guys like Ken Kelley, Steve Hickox, Derek Robichaud, Marco Rocca and the great PJ Dunphy of the Monoxides inspired me. Bands like Earth AD, Thee Suddens and The Varsity Weirdos kept a scene going when there wasn't one. Moncton legends like Jon Rockstar Flanagan, Nathan Jones, and Chris Lewis, who've worked their whole lives, dedicated to music: seeing their bands still touring and kicking ass inspires everyone.

And thanks to all those who make it happen behind the scenes, guys like Andrew Campbell, who helped developed the scene from the beginning. Ray 13, Shane Porter, Duane Kelly, Reuben Dupuis, Kyle

McDons, and everyone else who bought tickets, showed up to shows, lugged gear or bought a beer.

A huge thank you to Keith Morris (Black Flag/Off), Ian MacKaye (Minor Threat), Lee Ranaldo (Sonic Youth) and Steve McDonald (Redd Kross), and everyone else who helped make this book happen.

Moncton's music and arts scene has always defined itself with a do-it-yourself ethic. It may have started out of necessity and continued out of stubbornness, but it continues to exist because that's who we are: people who have something to say, want to share it with friends near and far, take the initiative, make something, and always relate with other people.

It continues at venues like the Esquire (RIP) and Claude's House, with bands like The Disasterbaters, Nerve Button, Mistreater, and Fear Agent.

To Moncton and the future, make it happen.

Finally, since most of this happened many moons ago and proper manners prevented me from ever passing on anything social, you might have to excuse the odd lapse in memory.

DISCOGRAPHY

ERIC'S TRIP
EPS/CASSETTES

- *Eric's Trip* cassette (Independent): December 1990

- *Catapillars* cassette (Independent): April 1991

- *Drowning* cassette (Independent): August 1991

- *Warm Girl* cassette (Independent): January 1992

- *Belong* 7" EP (NIM): April 1992

- *Peter* cassette (Murderecords) / LP (Sub Pop Germany): April 1993

- *Songs About Chris* 7" (4 songs) / CD (6 songs) (Sub Pop): May 1993

- *Julie and the Porthole to Dimentia* 7" (One solo track by each of the four members) (Sappy Records): July 1993

- *Warm Girl* 7" (Derivative): 1993

▌ *Trapped In New York* 7" (Summershine Records): 1994

▌ *The Gordon Street Haunting* 7" / CD (Sub Pop): 1994

▌ *The Road South* 7" (Sonic Unyon): August 1995

ALBUMS

▌ *Love Tara* LP/CD (Sub Pop): November 1993

▌ *Forever Again* LP/CD (Sub Pop): September 1994

▌ *Purple Blue* LP/CD (Sub Pop): January 1996

▌ *Long Days Ride 'Till Tomorrow* LP/CD (Sappy Records): October 1997

▌ *The Eric's Trip Show* live CD (Teenage USA): August 2001

▌ *Live in Concert November 4th, 2001* live CD (Great Beyond): 2002

▌ Bootleg LP (No Label): 2007

SPLITS

▌ "Laying Blame." Split 7" with Sloan (Cinnamon Toast Records): 1994

▌ "Pillow (Red)." Split 7" with Moviola (metoo! records): 1996

COMPILATIONS

▌ "Sickness." *Naked in the Marsh* 10" (NIM): 1991

▌ "Understanding." *Raw Energy* CD (Raw Energy Records): 1993

▌ "Blue Sky for Julie/Smother." *Never Mind the Molluscs* Double 7"/CD (Sub Pop): 1993

▌ "Blue Sky for Julie/Smother." *Sub Pop Employee of the Month* LP (Sub Pop): 1993

▌ "Laying Blame." *Trim Crusts if Desired* CD (Cinnamon Toast Records): 1994

/ "Evie." *Not If I Smell You First* CD (Sonic Unyon): August 1995

/ "If You Don't Want Me." *Teenage Zit Rock Angst* LP/CD/8-track (Nardwuar the Human Serviette/Mint Records): 1995

/ "So Easier Last Time." *More of Our Stupid Noise* (Squirtgun Records): 1996

/ "Fall (January 1996)." *Pet-kout-koy-ek: Songs For A River* CD (no label): 1996

/ "New Love" (remix) / "We're Only Gonna Die" (live in Montreal '94). *The Stareoscopic Scary Show* cassette (no label): 1997

ELEVATOR TO HELL

EPS

/ *Forward to Snow* 7" EP (Sappy Records): April 1995

/ *Backwards May* 7" (Sappy Records): September 1996

/ *Onwards and Away* 7" (Squirtgun): March 1997

ALBUMS

/ *Elevator to Hell* LP (Sub Pop): February 1995

/ *Part 3* 12" (Sub Pop): July 1996

/ *Parts 1–3* CD (Sub Pop): August 1996

/ *Eerieconsiliation* LP/CD (Sub Pop): August 1997

/ *Parts 4 and 5* cassette (Astronavigation): September 1997

/ *Original Music from the Motion Picture The Such* CD (Murderecords): May 1998

/ *Vague Premonition* LP / CD (Sub Pop / Sonic Unyon): April 1999

/ *Live in Concert April 24, 99* LP (Great Beyond): June 1999

/ *A Taste of Complete Perspective* LP / CD (Teenage USA) : September 2000

I *Early Band Recordings: February 1995–June 1997* CDR (Great Beyond): December 2001

I *Live in Concert 2001* CDR (Great Beyond): December 2001

I *Lost During Headquake* CDR (Great Beyond): December 2001

I *4D* CDR (Great Beyond): February 2002

I *Darkness → Light* CD (Blue Fog): October 2002

I *The Sightseer Project* CDR (Great Beyond): February 2003

I *Live in Toronto, October 24, 2003* CDR (Great Beyond): 2003

I *Parts Six and Seven* CDR (Great Beyond): Spring 2004

I *August* CD (Blue Fog): January 2005

COMPILATIONS

I "Over and Over." *The Stareoscopic Scary Show* cassette (no label): March 1996

I "Veins / Green." *More of Our Stupid Noise* CD (Squirtgun): July 1996

I "Deteriorate." *The Starioscopic Scary Show* (Extended Version) CD (no label): July 1997

I "The Cloud (live)." *The Vinyl Factory Vol. 1* LP (Music Manufacturing Services): October 1999

I "Gunningsville Drawbridge." *Syrup and Gasoline Vol.2* CD (Grenadine): July 2001

I "Thick Wall." *An Obscene Scene* CD (Hand Made Music): April 2003

I "The Current." *Snowsuit on and Heading North* CD (Out of Sound Records): November 2003

RICK WHITE

I *Notes From Stereo Mountain* 7" (Sub Pop): 1993

I *Perplexis Volume Seven* CDR (Great Beyond): 2001

I *Live at the Paramount Lounge, August 13, 2003* CDR (Great Beyond): 2003

I *The Unintended* (Rick White, Dallas Good, Greg Keelor, Mike Belitsky, Sean Dean and Travis Good) CD (Blue Fog): 2003

I *The Unintended / Constantines* Split LP (Blue Fog): 2005

I *The Rick White Album* LP (Blue Fog): September 2005

I *Memoreaper* LP (Blue Fog): May 2007

I *137* LP (Blue Fog): 2009

JULIE DOIRON

ALBUMS

I *Broken Girl* CD (Sub Pop, Sappy Records): 1996

I *Loneliest in the Morning* LP/CD (Sub Pop): 1997

I *Julie Doiron and the Wooden Stars* LP/CD (Tree Records, Sappy Records): 1999

I *Désormais* CD (Jagjaguwar, Endearing Records): 2001

I *Heart and Crime* LP/CD (Jagjaguwar, Endearing Records): 2002

I *Goodnight Nobody* LP/CD (Jagjaguwar, Endearing Records): 2004

I *Woke Myself Up* LP/CD (Jagjaguwar, Endearing Records): 2007

I *I Can Wonder What You Did with Your Day* (Jagjaguwar, Endearing Records): 2009

I *So Many Days* CD (Aporia Records): 2012

OTHER

I *Dog Love Part 2* 7" (as Broken Girl) (Sappy Records): 1993

I *Nora* 7" (as Broken Girl) (Sappy Records): 1995

I *Who will be the one* 7" (with the Wooden Stars) (Plumline): 1999

I *Will You Still Love Me?* (Tree Records, Sappy Records): 1999

I *Julie Doiron / Okkervil River* Split CD with Okkervil River (Acuarela): 2003

I *Lost Wisdom* (Mount Eerie with Julie Doiron and Frederick Squire) LP / CD (P.W. Elverum & Son): 2008

I "Oh Heavy Snow" / "It's Nice To Come Home." Split 7" with Calm Down It's Monday (K Records): 2009

I *Daniel, Fred & Julie* LP (with Daniel Romano and Frederick Squire) (You've Changed Records): 2009

I *Weird Lines* (Julie Doiron, Jon Mckiel, C.L. McLaughlin, James Anderson and Chris Meaney) LP (Sappy Records): July 2016

I *Homeless* (as Julie Doiron and the Wrong Guys) 7" (Wrong Guys Records): 2017

CHRIS THOMPSON

(Moonsocket)

ALBUMS

I *Moon Socket* cassette (Sappy Records): 1993

I *Socket to Me* cassette (Derivative Records): 1994

I *Moon Socket* CD (Derivative Records): 1995

I *The Best Thing* CD (Sappy Records): 1996

I *Take the Mountain* CD (Squirtgun Records): 1997

▌ *You Have a Pretty Life* CD (no label): 2011

▌ *Eurydice* LP (Noyes Records): 2015

EPS

▌ *Spaced-Odd-Ditties* 7" (Sappy Records): 1993

▌ *Moon Socket* 7" (Ratfish): 1995

▌ *Moon Socket* 7" (Sub Pop): 1995

▌ *It's the End of the Trip* 7" (Little Mafia) – 1997

(The Memories Attack, with Ron Bates)

ALBUMS

▌ *The Memories Attack* CD (no label): 2007

▌ *The Memories Attack* CD (Noyes Records): 2008

Everything

BIBLIOGRAPHY

This book was largely researched through face to face interviews with those who know the scene best: the musicians who created it. I talked to a wide variety of people about Eric's Trip, from Mark Gaudet to Ray Auffrey to Julie Doiron, and a ton of others who shared their experiences, like Ken Kelley, Chris Lewis, and Dana Robertson, who leant a ton of knowledge and experience about the good old days when the scene was new, young, and growing quick. These interviews were conducted from 2014 to 2017 in backyards, bars, and coffee shops in and around Moncton, New Brunswick.

Azerrad, Michael. *Our Band Could Be Your Life: Scenes from the American Indie Underground, 1981-1991.* New York: Back Bay Books, 2001.

Chart Attack. "Elevator To Hell: The Soapy Saga Of Eric's Trip And Elevator To Hell." *Chart Magazine*, March 1998. http://www.chartattack.com/news/1998/03/01/elevator-to-hell-the-soapy-saga-of-erics-trip-and-elevator-to-hell

▌ Gordon, Kim. *Girl in a Band*. New York: Dey Street Books, 2015.

▌ Jack, Ian A. D., Jason Schneider, and Michael Barclay. *Have Not Been the Same: The CanRock Renaissance 1985-1995*. Toronto: ECW Press, 2011.

▌ Khanna, Vish. "Eric's Trip: A Love Supreme." *EXCLAIM!* March 28, 2009. http://exclaim.ca/music/article/erics_trip-_love_supreme

▌ Lindsay, Cam. "22 Years Later, Eric's Trip Still 'Love Tara.'" *Noisey*. June 17, 2015. https://noisey.vice.com/en_ca/article/erics-trip-new-brunswick-love-tara-interview-2015

▌ McNeil, Legs, and McCain, Gillian. *Please Kill Me: The Uncensored Oral History of Punk*. New York: Grove Press, 2006.

▌ Mersereau, Bob. *The Top 100 Canadian Albums*. Fredericton, NB: Goose Lane Editions, 2007.

▌ Morris, Keith, with Ruland, Jim. *My Damage: The Story of a Punk Rock Survivor*. Boston: Da Capo Press, 2016.

▌ Paperheartmustic.net. "An Interview with Rick White." www.paperheartmusic.net/newsite/interview_rickwhite.htm

▌ Rollins, Henry. *Get in the Van: On the Road With Black Flag*. Los Angeles: 2.13.61 Publications, 1994.

▌ Smith, Patti. *Just Kids*. New York: HarperCollins, 2010.

▌ Sutherland, Sam. *Perfect Youth: The Birth of Canadian Punk*. Toronto: ECW Press, 2012.